FOOTBALL
FOR WEEKEND WARRIORS

FOOTBALL
FOR WEEKEND WARRIORS

A GUIDE TO EVERYTHING FROM TOUCHDOWNS
TO TORN TENDONS TO TAILGATING

RANDY HOWE

THE LYONS PRESS
Guilford, Connecticut
An imprint of The Globe Pequot Press

The Lyons Press is an imprint of The Globe Pequot Press.

10 9 8 7 6 5 4 3 2 1

Printed in the United States of America

Designed by Maggie Peterson

ISBN 1-59228-803-0

Library of Congress Cataloging-in-Publication data is available on file.

To Buddy Jobin
and anyone else who's ever tried to teach
the kids of Kisco the Wing-T offense.

Acknowledgments

A debt of gratitude to . . .
Rob, for being the editorial equivalent of a pulling guard.
Willie, for lending me the latest in AV technology.
Al, BVA, Eric, Joe, Dr. John, Mike, Paul, and Nutsy,
for being such super supermodels!
And finally, Alicia, for not only tolerating my athletic
infatuations but encouraging them.

Disclaimer

I was the kicker.

Prelude

Tight spirals and tight coverage.

Green grass outside of the hash marks; mud, sweat, and tears within.

Gatorade over the head, ice and all.

Sitting on the tailgate of your buddy's truck before the game.

Cheerleaders, foam fingers, beer, and brats. The safety blitz.

A running back hit so hard his mouthguard is sent flying like they were the teeth themselves.

Long arms stretching to haul in the Hail Mary.

The offensive line of the Dallas Cowboys breaking huddle and like synchronized swimmers rising then dropping down into the three-point stance. As one. Tony Dorsett off to the races.

Terry Bradshaw heaving the ball from his heels and Lynn Swan or John Stallworth (pick your poison) leaping to make an immaculate reception of their own.

The *Sports Illustrated* poster of James Lofton leaping.

Walter Payton's *Sports Illustrated* poster, too. Oh, Sweetness . . . The close-up on Wilbur Marshall's eyes. The wide-angle view of Fridge's end zone celebration.

Phil Simms converting third and eighteen. Mark Bavaro carrying men on his back like they were children. LT.[1]

Joe Montana rolling to his right and "finding" Dwight Clark in the back of the end zone. Ronnie Lott finding himself without part of his finger so that he could play in the Super Bowl.

---

[1] *Just think about this for a minute: he could've been even better . . .*

The Icky Shuffle.

Doug Flutie to Gerard Phelan, to give Boston College its greatest victory ever.

Dan Marino, John Elway, Brett Favre, and all those other NRA quarterbacks.

Bo running over The Boz and then running all the way into the tunnel.

Deion Sanders single-handedly slaughtering the Giants on *Monday Night Football*. Despite throwing up in the end zone.

Peyton audiblizing.

Vinatieri splitting snowflakes and then the uprights.

Paul threading the needle.

Mike running a crisp pattern to earn the first down (while wearing his lucky Chrebet jersey).

Nutsy down on one knee, but still blocking.

My body a heavy weight on the bed, pillows under the knees and heating pad beneath the back.

And all because the only thing better than watching football . . . is playing football.

Table of Contents

From the Webster's Old School Dictionary

game[1] (gām) *noun* **1** any form of play or way of playing; amusement; recreation; sport **2** any specific contest, engagement, self-injurious behavior involving a score, other players, beer, trash talk, scabs, sweat, and physical feats of mind-over-matter **3** a way or quality of playing in competition **4** any test of skill, courage, or endurance **5** wild animals hunted and killed and cooked over an open flame before the coin toss

game[2] (gām) *adjective* **1** to be lame or injured

Introduction

Putting the Warrior Back into Weekend Warrior

For eighteen months I rotted away. I was like a broken trophy, curled up in the fetal position at the bottom of an equipment bag that nobody bothers to open anymore. I was old before my time. Fat, too.

As many of you have experienced, I'd been shelved by an injury. After trying to play baseball again, I herniated my L5S1 and came within a day of back surgery. The neurosurgeon said to just take it easy, give it time, and see what happens, but I am good at doing none of these things. I like to see what's happening while I'm *doing* it. If I've got time to give, I'm gonna give it to my boys on the field of play. Taking it easy is for those who like it easy: nice and easy and neat and clean. It's for those who like no sweat, no dirt, no competition, and no gridiron.

Not much fun and definitely not the life for me.

But there I was with a heating pad on my back every night and doing a whole lot of stretching and strengthening during the day. Sometimes a hiatus offers opportunity for reflection, and as the reflection staring back at me from the mirror packed on the pounds, I saw a former player who desperately wanted to get back onto the football field. It was time to put the warrior back into weekend warrior!

Naturally, I wondered if it would ever really happen. Even those who don't worry much must ask themselves, Have I played my last game? Am I really done? Is it time for shuffleboard, senior discounts, and dentures? For me, the answer was no.

Words cannot describe how happy I was this past fall when I was finally able to play pain-free again. And like riding a bike, it all came back to me. After a couple of tentative patterns, I remembered how important it is to sell it one way before juking another; I felt the thrill of the well-concealed blitz; I broke on a pass, dove through the air like I was seven again, and the opposition's dreams of converting a fourth-and-six were dashed as I knocked the ball to the ground.[2] I threw a duck or two, but mixed a tight spiral in for a touchdown. And team confidence meant that when we got the ball back it was my finger designing a play on Nutsy's belly. The heat of battle . . . the thrill of the fight . . . football!!!

So good was the game that when I tried to leave early for some domestic duty, I didn't mind one bit their refusal to let me go. I'd forgotten about peer pressure and how it's not always a bad thing. We like to be talked into fun, to have our rubber arms twisted. There is a catchphrase bandied about by my boys and on that first day, I heard it loud and clear: "One more trip up and back?" A question that isn't really a question at all.

Guaranteed, these words are spoken at least once every time we play.[3] There's always some poor sap who's supposed to leave earlier but gets dragged back into it for another fifteen minutes. "Come on, now . . . One more trip up and back?" "All right. But that's it. Seriously." Yep, seriously.

---

[2] *I'd even remembered to not intercept it, as they'd be turning the ball over on downs and it was better to be fifteen yards upfield, at the original line of scrimmage. Like riding a bike . . .*

[3] *"Just five more minutes," "One more set of downs for each," and "Get your butt back on the field!" are some other possible taunts/offers.*

Nothing sums up the football mentality—especially when it comes to gainfully employed, child-rearing, lawn-mowing, in-law humoring weekend warriors—better than this phrase. The response is preordained, so get used to it. Like the proposition of a press in golf, no man can deny these kinds of offers. They are a means to extend the game: a way to put off the yard work or whatever else awaits in the real world. It's confirmation that you are once again an athlete, that you have (re)entered the world of the weekend warrior.

Football is a game that invites you to play as hard as you want, sweat as profusely as possible, and leave as much as you can on the field. At our age, no one will get on you for dogging it. (Well, maybe just a little . . .) It's gotten so hard to rally the troops that just by showing up you will be appreciated. Our game is two-hand touch, and no, I don't miss the days of tackle at all. Our brand of pickup pigskin is like getting a new CD without having to take off that security tape at the top; it's like ordering a Guinness and having it arrive five seconds later rather than five minutes; like adopting a dog and discovering that she's already housebroken and can fetch you the remote control. Two-hand touch is all the benefits without the bodily harm: the fun of football without the broken bones.

Not to say I'm anything less than paralyzingly sore after a game. I am! I am!!! But it's a good feeling, definitely much better than simply feeling fat.

I am fortunate that, despite being a father and having two jobs, I still have time for "One more trip up and back?" I am fortunate in that I have a place to play and guys to play with. Four years ago we moved to Madison from New York and I fell in with a bunch of likeminded fellows. These are guys who will get up at eight A.M. on a Sunday morning to shoot hoops. They'll get up even earlier to squeeze in eighteen holes before lunch. These are

Just short of the lacrosse goal-turned-first down marker, Eric two-hands hard enough to keep BVA from hauling this one in (see ball popping loose above their heads!).

guys who are willing to risk injury, and reinjury, to line it up between the hash marks on a cold December day; who will leave the house at eleven o'clock on a Tuesday night because that's the only available ice time; who will take lessons just so they can move up the tennis ladder; who push the office chair *away* from the trash can just to see if they can make it from three-point land; and whose ears perk up at the mere mention of an outing, game, or match. These are men who become boys at the drop of a hat, puck, and putt.

And there are people like this in just about every town across America. These are folks who love their children, their spouses, their boyfriends, girlfriends, and pets, but who really, really *love* their games. And given the chance to play, they find a way. We weekend warriors will always find a way.

Some of you may be reading this after one too many post patterns, or on the Wednesday night before the family's annual

Turkey Bowl. For you, I need not say more. You're already hooked. You're already in touch with the touchdowns and tail-gating and torn tendons. But for those of you who've been away for a while, just know that there's a group of guys out there who need you: that somebody is scrambling left then right then left again, desperately looking downfield for an open man. You could be that man.

And worst-case scenario, if you're already an addict but are laid up, trying to take it easy, just give it time and see what hap-pens—do everything you can to get back out there. Work for it. Do not deny the athlete that still resides within. Like I said, every game needs players. The more guys who come out, the better it will be. *You* could be the one to turn a small-time game into something more. A four-on-four? A five-on-five? Anything is possible when people say yes. Momentum starts with one.

There are no field goals, no helmets, no cheerleaders, and no zebras. Just you and your boys with the breath streaming out of your mouths and the steam rising off of your heads. Sandwich bags on your feet and grippy gloves on your hands. A blitz that catches them by surprise. A razzle-dazzle like you read about. This is the essence of weekend warrior football. This is why, when you announce you've got to get going, you're admittedly happy to hear "One more trip up and back?" nobody's ready to accept your resignation. Not quite yet. Rather, there's a group of men-turned-boys huddled up and waiting for you to join them on the march to victory and another on the other side of the ball just dying to stand in your way. Hike.

1

From Schoolboy Soccer to 300-Pound Linemen: A Historical Look at the Game We Love

While researching this book, I learned that the history of stupidity in the name of football fun goes all the way back to the seventeenth century. It was in 1638 that eight Brits—hearty young men I would've been proud to call friends—were playing soccer on the frozen surface of the River Trent when the ice broke.[1] In the years following the drowning incident, soccer was illegal, but people, especially working-class boys, still found ways to play. Britain's brain trust even went a step further, deciding to make soccer more violent (i.e., fun!),

[1] *Makes Stanford's marching band look bright by comparison, doesn't it?*

and this is how football's other ancestor, rugby, came to be. Rugby was the game of choice not just for the poor but also the wealthy, and was soon the most widely played game at Britain's boarding schools. One was even called The Rugby School.

Each school played by their own rules until Cambridge University established an official set of rules in 1848. The biggest benefit of this was that the schools could now play one another. Next thing you know, "College Game Day" is setting up outside of fraternity houses and Vegas is providing the lines for everything from coin tosses to how many cartwheels the Penn State drum major will do.

Debate of the rules continued as love of the game grew. One area of debate was the practice of "hacking"—the act of kicking the opponent in the shins "in order to convince him to drop the ball." Rules committees quickly realized that the best way to keep everyone happy was to recognize two different games. And so rugby and soccer were officially separated in 1863. Who could've guessed there would be a third sport born of these first two?

Years before, soccer had hopped aboard the *Mayflower* in search of freedom from persecution—meaning mainly shin guards and yellow cards!—and quickly found a home in the New World. "Colonists kicked and threw," the Professional Football Researchers Association's (PFRA) reports, "inflated bladders or sawdust-filled leather balls around long before they decided to fire on the whites of the redcoats' blue eyes." And this is where we find the origin of the word "pigskin." Those inflated bladders were often borrowed (like when a friend asks to "borrow" some toilet paper . . .) from a pig, at least until Charles Goodyear went into business for himself. According to Cecil Adams, author of *The Straight Dope*, vulcanized rubber meant rubber balls and the end to pigskin. At least in the literal sense.

On that note, Adams also shared that the name for the shape of a football is a "prolate spheroid." This is officially defined as "round but pointy."

A rugby ball is also a prolate spheroid and like rugby, football was cultivated in the finest educational institutions in the land. At Harvard, "Bloody Monday" was the first day of each new college year and featured the freshman and sophomore classes beating each other mercilessly. In that PFRA article, there was a classic exaggeration of an observation: "Had 15-yard penalties been handed out, it is conceivable they would have reached California." Apparently, hacking was big on both sides of the Big Pond. Harvard's freshmen kicked the ball well and the sophomores kicked well, too. Unfortunately, it was the freshmen they were kicking! I tell you, games played with animal bladders . . . Victorians kicking Victorians . . . Valedictorians kicking valedictorians . . . If only all history were this interesting!!!

Even after Harvard banned the game—anything worth doing, it seems, has to be illegal at one point or another—boys would gather on Saturday afternoons, playing their version of soccer on the Boston Common. A few years later, it was only bacon that pigs were makin', as rubber balls came into play and laws regarding the game were loosened. Soccer was reinstated at the colleges, but the more football-like games were still outlawed for fear of injury, rabble-rousing, and Lee Corso's jokes. The first intercollegiate soccer game took place in New Jersey in 1869 with Rutgers playing Princeton. At the very same time, James Naismith was a schoolboy and dreaming up the game of basketball. (Like football, his game would be developed as a way of keeping young men actively engaged and out of trouble.) Years later, the Basketball Hall of Fame would open its doors in Springfield, Massachusetts, and it was in New Haven, less than one hundred miles south, that Walter Camp invented football as we know it today.

You may recognize the name, as the Walter Camp Award is handed out to the best Division I college football player every year. It was while at Yale—Camp matriculated in 1876—that the Elis joined the Intercollegiate Football Association (IFA), a grouping of Ivy League schools interested in beating the crap out of each other. The game they played was Britain's version of rugby, moving away from soccer and embracing the raw energy and violence that still marks final exams, I mean football, today. Between 1878 and 1925, Camp participated in the intercollegiate legislatures that determined the number of points that would be awarded for touchdowns and the number of players allowed on the field (the number was dropped from fifteen to eleven), and it was he who oversaw the evolution of the game with an eye for detail and the heart of a lion. Or, more aptly, the brains of an Eli. For example, Camp argued against the rugby scrum. He wanted more plotting and planning in the game. More strategy and less kill the carrier! No doubt, he would have disapproved of the Bengals' no-huddle offense during the Boomer Esiason era.

In promoting the elimination of the scrum, Camp wrote: "A scrimmage takes place when the holder of the ball puts it on the ground before him and puts it in play while on-side either by kicking the ball or by snapping it back with his foot. The man who first receives the ball from the snap-back shall be called the quarter-back and shall not rush forward with the ball under penalty of foul." Just like that, the man had invented the line of scrimmage and the quarterback![2]

---

[2] *And being the smart fellows that they were, they figured out pretty quick that kicking the ball back was a stupid idea.*

It was around this time that each of the positions was given a name. Next-to-ends evolved into tackles because they usually recorded the most tackles. The men on either side of the center were charged with guarding him as he snapped the ball, so they were guards. I have no idea why running backs were named running backs, though.

Now that there was a line of scrimmage but no scrum, a rule was needed for unforced turnovers. So, Camp wrote, "If on three consecutive fairs and downs a team shall not have advanced the ball five yards, nor lost ten, they must give up the ball to opponents at the spot of the fourth down." This was on October 12, 1882, the date now widely recognized as the birth of American football. Before this day there was no third and long. No "You going for it?" and no turned-over-on-downs. Bye-bye, soccer. Best o' luck, rugby. Hellooooo, football!!!

Football Facts

Back in the day, somebody remarked that the 110-yard-long fields—marked every five yards, as that was considered a first down—looked like a "gridiron." This nickname for football fields is made even more appropriate by the fact that a gridiron is a metal framework for broiling or grilling meat. Like at a tailgate!

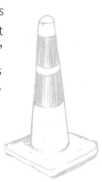

In 1899, the Morgan Athletic Club football team was formed on the south side of Chicago. The team changed names to the Normals, then the Cardinals, and also changed locations, from Morgan to Racine to Chicago to St. Louis to Phoenix, and then finally to Arizona, thus making the Arizona Cardinals the oldest franchise in American football history. And franchises were springing up not in the most unlikely of places, necessarily, but from the most unlikely of sources. Including baseball teams! In 1902, Philadelphia's two professional baseball teams, the Phillies and the Athletics, started up football teams to compete against the Pittsburgh Stars. The Stars, incidentally, had a fullback by the name of Christy Mathewson.[3] These Keystone Staters called their league the National Football League, but the NFL as we know it would not be officially formed for another eighteen years.

Although Camp was making his changes in the East, the game grew out of western Pennsylvania and Ohio. The Great War meant big business in these blue-collar states, and all of a sudden people had money to spend on leisure activities, especially professional sports.[4] You can thank these folks for letting owners know that pigskin was popular enough to make their investments worthwhile, but you can also thank that most native of Americans, Jim Thorpe.

Thorpe was the running backs coach at Indiana University when the Canton Bulldogs offered him big money to come and play against archrival Massillon. Two weeks later, not only was Thorpe the team's best player, he was also the coach! Thorpe quickly proved himself to be the best kicker and also the best "thrower" of his day. But it was as a running back that he really shined. According to the PFRA website, "His favorite running

---

[3] *Mathewson is a member of baseball's Hall of Fame.*
[4] *Also, in 1913, Knute Rockne and Notre Dame had beaten Army, helping to propel the game to national prominence.*

trick in an open field was to lower his shoulder and charge straight at a defender. Then at the moment of impact, he would lift and 'peel back' the defender." Peel back: that's the kind of palpable expression that makes football a joy to play, watch, read about, and yes, research!

Thorpe was Bo Jackson and Deion Sanders long before those two inked their first contract. He won gold medals in the pentathlon and decathlon at the 1912 Olympics and had played baseball for the New York Giants. If he played in the 1990s, by now he'd be an analyst for Fox, have a reality show on MTV, and collectors everywhere would be on eBay bidding up Jim Thorpe bobblehead dolls.

Another noteworthy player in the early days of the NFL was Byron White. Yes, Byron White, the same man who went on to become a justice on the United States Supreme Court. (Football had come a long way since the days of the River Trent!) Before donning the black robe, he wore the black and gold of the University of Colorado in both football and basketball. After college, Art Rooney drafted him to the Pittsburgh Pirates—soon to be renamed the Steelers—of the ten-team NFL. White led the league in rushing, and it wouldn't be the last of his successes. After being sold to the Lions, White went to Yale Law School where he was able to study during the week and play football on the weekends, thus making him the original weekend warrior! He served in the Navy during World War II, and two decades later joined the Supreme Court.

Speaking of the war, it was in 1944 that the All-American Football Conference was formed. Although never officially associated with the American Football League (AFL), a progression was followed that eventually led to the merger of the AFL and NFL. The AAFC was short-lived, but introduced the country to franchises like the Bills, the Colts, the Bears, the Seahawks, the

49ers, and the Browns, who were considered to be the league's best team. Oh, how the mighty have fallen . . .

Before I forget, let's take a moment to discuss the eyesore of professional football. No, I don't mean Kurt Warner's wife. I mean the Pro Bowl.

In 1951, the Pro Bowl was revived at the Los Angeles Coliseum.[5] This time, it was a battle between the American and National Conferences. Unfortunately, the annual game is still being played today. All too often, Pro Bowlers back out with exaggerated injuries, fake funerals, and the ever-popular "previous commitment," forcing the three diehard fans who actually tune in to watch the Saints' water boy guard a Raiderette! The game is a waste, with fans still talking about the Super Bowl but ready for March Madness and spring training. Perhaps if the game was a bunch of smaller games . . . My idea is to bring back a format similar to ABC's fine show of the 1970s, *Battle of the Network Stars*. Except that in this case it could be announcers in the dunk tank while linemen throw the football at the little circular target. I'd tune in to watch Madden get wet! I might even tune in to see a potato sack race pairing owners and players. Who wouldn't want to see Michael Strahan dragging one of the ancient Maras down the field? I propose a pie-eating contest between failed first-round picks from years past and for the grand finale, a tug-of-war between the long snappers of the AFC and NFC. Fantastic!

So, the 1950s began with the reincarnation of the Pro Bowl and ended with the debut of one of the game's finest minds. It was in 1959 that Vince Lombardi was named coach of the Green Bay Packers, but this news was overshadowed by the first draft of the AFL. The league was the idea of Dallas owner Lamar Hunt, and teams from Denver, Houston, Los Angeles, Minneapolis, New

[5] *The game had been inaugurated in 1939 as a battle between the NFL champs (my Giants!) and a team of All Stars, but was quickly abandoned.*

York, Buffalo, and Boston decided to give the NFL a run for its money. In its inaugural year, 1960, AFL games were played on Friday nights so as to not compete against Saturday's college games and Sunday's NFL matchups. Getting a TV contract helped the AFL to succeed where the AAFC had failed, and on New Year's Day, 1961, the Houston Oilers beat the Los Angeles Chargers in the first-ever AFL championship game.

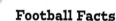

Football Facts

According to writer Mel Bashore, the smallest guy to ever play in the NFL was Jack "Soapy" Shapiro. Soapy only played one game, in 1929, returning a kick for twelve yards, but it's worth noting that he was only five foot one and weighed just 119 pounds. Some other notable "big" men include Nate Abrams (5'4", 145 pounds), Ray Brenner (5'5", 145 pounds), Dick Dobeleit (5'4", 155 pounds), Patsy Giugliano (5'4", 140 pounds), Ed Gregg (5'6", 135 pounds), Two Bits Homan (5'5", 145 pounds), and a fellow with a rather appropriate last name, Butch Meeker (5'3", 143 pounds). It also bears mentioning that none of these guys played after 1950, generally considered the start of the "modern era" of football.

In 1963, the National Football Hall of Fame opened its doors in Canton, Ohio, and two years later football overtook the "National Pastime" as America's favorite sport. According to a Harris survey, football received an approval rating of 41 percent, while baseball received just 38 percent of the vote. Not satisfied to rest on their laurels, professional football's owners decided to take it to the next level. And so it was that on June 8, 1966, the two professional football leagues combined forces. The merger was on. Pete Rozelle shared the news with the media, including the announcement of the AFL-NFL World Championship Game, to be played in January of 1967. Order up a keg and six-foot wedge, boys. There's big-time football to be watched!

The Packers sent the Chiefs packin', 35–10, and the following year the game was played again, but under a different name: Super Bowl II. A tradition had been born.

Vince Lombardi, the man for whom the Super Bowl trophy is named, died of cancer in 1970. Lombardi is now the yardstick by which all other coaches are measured. Jim Thorpe may be on par with Apollo, but Lombardi is Zeus. Still an icon today, thirty-five years after his passing, he is where all coaching discussions begin and end. Before he's done, Bill Belichick might be considered the greatest, but right now only one other coach from recent memory even comes close: Don Shula. His career record was 347-173-6—for the Colts and Dolphins—and he was the last coach to lead a team to an undefeated season.

Although I never did root for his Fish, the 1970s seemed to be the heyday for football. It was during this time that I really began to love the sport. In addition to playing, I killed I don't know how many hours in class drawing helmets, the circular symbol of the Steel Curtain, Roger Staubach's star, the jet, the bolt, the oil rig, the eagle's wing, the patriotic center, Steve Largent's seahawk, the bronco bucking his way out of the "D," the horn of the purple people eater, and even the most intimidating of designs, the dolphin jumping through the hoop. Flipper was a fullback, I think.[6]

In 1976, New Jersey's Meadowlands welcomed my beloved Giants, allowing them to escape from the orange and royal blue hues of Shea Stadium. And perhaps it was blackmail—the Maras threatening to reveal they'd found Jimmy Hoffa's remains beneath a Jacuzzi—that allowed the team to retain its New York name.

Although I love the Giants, my earliest memories of football are of the Super Bowl and, in particular, the Pittsburgh Steelers. Every NFL Films production I ever saw seemed to feature the acrobatics of Lynn Swann and John Stallworth, the acting skills of Mean Joe Greene, the quiet competence of Mike Webster, and the rumbling, stumbling, ground-gaining rampages of Franco Harris. Of course we can't forget the lovable leader, Terry "I'm Banging the Lipton Soup Ice Skater Chick" Bradshaw. What's it all add up to? For this elementary schooler, it added up to football's finest era.

Then came the 1980s, beginning with the Super Bowl blunders of Vince Ferragamo. Steelers win again. And wacky stuff happened, like the other New York team—meaning *New York City*, Bills' fans—moving into Giants Stadium. The Jets are still there today, but a lot is happening with that West Side Stadium deal. I wonder whose body will end up in the foundation should it ever be built. Saddam Hussein would be nice, for starters. Plant him in one end zone and Osama Bin Jackass in the other. What better tribute to Ground Zero could there be?

Speaking of politics, in 1985 Ronald Reagan was sworn in for his second term before San Francisco defeated Shula's hoop-jumping Dolphins in the Super Bowl. The Gipper watched

---

[6] *No, wait—that was Larry Csonka!*

alongside 115,936,000 other people, making Super Bowl XIX the most widely viewed television event in the history of mankind, womankind, and any other kind you can think of. During big games, I like to imagine famous people doing the exact same thing I'm doing. For instance, Bono scarfing down a chicken wing just as I am. Pass the bleu cheese, B! Or how about Pamela Anderson reaching for a Coors Light as I reach for a Silver Bullet of my own? Ray Romano buying up the last eighteen boxes in the pool; Paula Abdul ordering a Hawaiian pizza as I whisper sweet nothings into the phone (how else can you get a delivery in less than four hours on Super Bowl Sunday?!); Condi Rice grabbing the remote so as to avoid the halftime show, her well-manicured finger pressing the button for the both of us.

Nobody turned the channel on the Chicago Bears, though. With The Fridge, Jim McMahon, Mike Ditka, and the rest, this team had more personality than they knew how to handle. And more scoring options, too, especially when it came to Super Bowl XX. Those weren't Belichick's Pats getting abused like that! But how could anybody hope to beat a team capable of producing a quality tune like "The Super Bowl Shuffle"?

The 1990s gave me another Giants' Super Bowl victory as the Bills and Scott Norwood took over for the Broncos in the role of victim. But soon it would be another NFC East team's turn to claim dominance—a dominance like the Giants have never known.[7] Emmitt, Troy, Michael, and the old man, Bill Bates, earned Jerry Jones three Super Bowl championships in a span of four years. On the flip side, Buffalo's luck never improved, shackling them with the unfair legacy of "loser," despite a dominance of their own over AFC opponents. But they were forced to play whipping boy to Jimmy Johnson's Boys and helped create another

[7] We don't have cheerleaders, either. I ask you, where's the justice?

generation of star-drawing youth. Ah, the Cowboys, America's team. Those darlings of network TV. And you can't talk about football and TV without mentioning *Monday Night Football*. So there, I mentioned it.[8]

I should also mention the game's latest and greatest dynasty. In three of the last four seasons, the New England Patriots have brought the trophy home to Foxboro. Although they are now *the* team to beat, the challengers are coming from here, there, and everywhere. For example, their opponent was different in each of the games, as they beat the Rams, Panthers, and Eagles. Moreso than any other sport, the NFL is enjoying a renaissance in parity, and every team stands a chance when preseason ends and the regular season begins. Even my Giants!

---

[8] *ESPN now has the rights to MNF and is planning on flexible scheduling, in the hopes of avoiding a late-season matchup of the 2-12 Saints and 1-13 Cardinals. Brilliant!*

2

The "Not Quite Ready for Canton Players": The Partellows, Pigskin, and Big Bird

One of my fondest childhood memories is staying up late for *Saturday Night Live* and the "Not Quite Ready for Prime Time Players." Belushi and Martin are certainly worthy of a television Hall of Fame and in the same vein, there are several people out there who belong in my personal pigskin Hall of Fame. Aykroyd, Chase, and Radner all showed me what funny is, just as a number of neighbors, coaches, and friends taught me about football, giving me a greater appreciation of the game and of sports in general. For their efforts, these "Not Quite Ready for Canton Players" will be recognized in a paperback that retails for less than a jock. Now that's what I call a tribute.

This addiction of mine started long before I watched my Giants win two Super Bowls (from the couch), long before I watched my high school team win two Bowl championships (from the bench!), and long before my Pop Warner team won two league championships. My love of football has its roots between the curbs of Marion Avenue. That's right, the seeds were planted in concrete—Dad and me versus the Partellows. Big Myles and Little Myles were all about running fly patterns from one end of the street to the other, while all Dad and I could muster was the occasional three-yard down and out.

Dad had been a punter and I would be a punter.[9] On the flip side, Little Myles would have a police record before his sixteenth birthday! We didn't stand a chance until another neighbor made a guest appearance. The high school quarterback lived up the road and decided to join us after witnessing a particularly pitiful set of downs. Dave Hughes, *the* Dave Hughes, the starting QB Dave Hughes, made a crack about Dad maybe having better luck playing on *Sesame Street*, but made up for it by joining our cause. "Run some routes, Big Bird, and lemme throw a couple."

Little Myles and Big Myles didn't stand a chance. Danette, neither.

Danette Partellow was the blonde bombshell who first showed me there was life outside of sports. Watching her steam up a variety of car windows at night, I had an inkling of what my future desires would be. But on that Friday afternoon, all of the desire I had in my body was focused on football and winning. I think all that Dave desired was Danette! And what better way to impress her than shredding the entire family with his passes?

Having Dave and Danette in the game meant my little brother Chuck was invited to play as well. This was the kind of

[9] *A kicker, too, but so as to not totally discredit myself, I also played tight end and defensive end. The sleeve of my jacket looked like an eye chart!*

spontaneous fun that people used to have before playdates. Mothers didn't need Palm Pilots; they had dinner bells, or whistles, or voices loud enough to draw their loin fruit home.[10] There just doesn't seem to be much unstructured, go-scar-your-knees free-time play these days. Gone are the days of concrete and curb football. There are no more down and outs, even if the down-and-out is the dejected feeling after a loss. Far sadder than losing, though, is the fact that little boys don't get to guard big girls anymore. For instance, Chuck got the thrill of his life when Danette turned upfield after a catch and he mistakenly, blissfully two-hand touched her right on her pom-poms! My thrill came with a down and out just over the goal line (from the fire hydrant on one side to the telephone pole on the other). Dave's pass hit me in the hands and my feet stopped just short of the curb so as to stay in bounds. Big Bird had to be happy for both of his sons as we all returned to the nest.

A few months later, he would be the proud papa once more as Chuck and I won his office Super Bowl pool. The following year, somebody decided it was unethical to let kids bet, so we were out of luck. We never beat the Partellows again either, but we'd managed to gain a little bit of pride, earn some of that Super Bowl cash, and Chuck, at the ripe old age of seven, had enjoyed a glimpse of manhood, all compliments of the great game of football.

Soon thereafter, Danette left for college and we put our house on the market. My Dad had a new job and couldn't play as much, and the Partellows were about to get divorced. Little Myles was into girls and petty crime. The only quality time Chuck and I got with Dave was when he'd try to run us down after work. Screaming "Car! Car! C! A! R!!!" we'd scatter like flushed quail, jumping that curb just a split second before Dave's tow truck roared by.

---

[10] *You'd never leave the game right away, though. This was just the first warning. When she called again, that was number two. And once the screen door slammed shut, game over!*

The neighborhood would grow quiet again—at least until the screen door slammed shut for dinner.

And the inductees are . . .
Little Myles (for going 99-1 in football, Wiffle Ball, and all things Atari), Dave Hughes (for going 1-0), and Big Bird (for being a great Dad).

3

The Way We Play: First and Thirty-Three

As kids, we struggled more with deciding what to play than with how to play it. Once we'd settled upon a game, be it Freeze Tag, Ghosts in the Graveyard, HORSE, Wiffle Ball, or the aforementioned concrete and curb football, determining the rules was a piece of cake.

Can you imagine the chaos if fair play wasn't a motivating factor for kids? Weekend warriors are kids at heart, and that includes everything from playing till the screen door slams to having a healthy respect for the rules. It's a good thing too, as several of the scenarios below could very well happen without them.

CHAOS AND THE "ON THE SPOT" RULES COMMITTEE

1. "I say we just let it go this time," says the defensive back after using a lasso, electrical tape, and a bear trap to tackle the receiver before the quarterback has even released the ball. "I agree!" says everyone on his team.
2. "We oughta get the ball at the spot, plus a free kick at your shins! Long live hacking!!!" cries the same guy when he's the victim of pass interference.
3. "Offsides? But I counted 'two Mississippi' and 'three Mississippi' . . . in my head," says the defensive lineman after rushing two counts too early.
4. "Make it, take it?" the end zone–dancing receiver suggests, hoping to bring a little bit of pickup hoops to the pigskin party (and get back on offense as soon as possible).
5. And the heady offensive lineman, when called for holding, shrugs innocently and says, "It was a hug. I just wanted to show you how much I care. You can't penalize a guy for caring!"

But there are some legitimate debates that take place on the field. To help prepare you, here are three that I learned about this past "season." (Answers at the bottom.)

1. Is it legal to have the quarterback say Hike, but then the center snaps the ball to the running back?
2. What is the penalty when a receiver sets a pick?
3. Is the offense allowed to send two wide-outs in motion at the same time?[11]

---

[11] *1. Nope, not legal. The penalty is a loss of down and the ball returns to the spot where the running back caught it. 2. Unless it's a blatant (and painful!) pick by the receiver, this is usually a no-call. 3. No, sir. But the penalty is minimal. Usually, the decision is "Automatic do-over," as more likely than not both receivers thought the QB was talking to him in the huddle!*

It's so much better to know the rules than to have to deal with situations "on the spot." This is a general rule for life and a specific necessity for football. Besides, after spending all week mixing it up at work, who wants to argue on a Saturday morning? When it's forty degrees and raining, do you really want to stand around debating illegal motion? If you and your boys spend too much time talking and not enough playing, the following overview of the rules might be of help; tailor to your needs as we have and then get back to the game. There's a reason kids don't spend a lot of time debating rules: it isn't as much fun as playing!

The NIRSA (National Intramural-Recreational Sports Association) rules are generally accepted, from college to adult rec leagues, as the standard. The folks who run the University of Florida's intramural sports program follow NIRSA's guidelines pretty closely, and here are some of the rules that might be of use to you and yours:

1. "The field dimensions are eighty yards by forty yards with ten-yard end zones." This is about right for our games. Of course, we go shorter if we've only got a three-on-three. Whatever the field's length, we put pylons at the halfway point for a first down. One first down per trip and that's it.

2. "Play at the beginning of each half will start at the offense's fourteen-yard line." We only pace off seven yards.[12] Also, we don't play with a clock or halves. The game starts when it starts and ends when someone keels over and revisits his breakfast.

3. "The referee's decisions are final in all matters pertaining to the game." No, we don't have referees and chances are neither do you (unless you're lucky enough to be in an organized flag

[12] *The same when a team decides to "punt," as we don't do any actual kicking or punting.*

Al and BVA run crisp routes as they both buttonhook just beyond the lacrosse goal for the potential first down (we had no pylons that day).

football league). So, we've all got to regulate ourselves. As a general rule I find that in football as in basketball, it's best to simply say, "Respect the call" and move on. Besides, the only thing that ever gets called is pass interference. In regards to contact at the line, we allow bumping within five yards of the line while the U of F does not: "During a down in which a legal forward pass crosses the offensive line of scrimmage, contact or action that interferes with an eligible receiver who is beyond the line of scrimmage is pass interference."

4. "Each team must provide their own football." We like to keep our princessy quarterbacks happy, so whatever ball he wants to use . . .

5. "All intramural participants are responsible for their own medical expenses." This must fill the U of F parents with confidence. Right up there with hearing, "My butt is still a little sore from pledging." I've included this rule because you

Without that white jersey, Dr. John might get lost in the background, brown vest against brown trees and track. And worse, if the guy guarding him is wearing dark colors, how'm I gonna know who to throw to?!?![13]

are obviously responsible for your own co-pay, even if a fellow player chips your tooth, like I did to my buddy Mike this past winter. My apologies, Mike.

6. "All team members must wear the same shade of color shirt." Dark versus light is the going rate. Paul provides the pinnies just like he does the pylons.

7. "Players may carry a Play Book inside their clothing as long as it is not made of unyielding material." There are some serious flag football leagues out there. It just isn't where I happen to be coming from.

8. "Shoes with metal, ceramic, screw-in, or detachable cleats" are considered illegal. The only equipment request I've ever been witness to is one guy being asked to remove his watch.

---

[13] *I believe it was Vinnie TestesVerde who claimed to be color-blind. And this was while playing for the bright orange Buccaneers!*

9. "Failure to snap within twenty-five seconds after the ball is whistled ready for play." We have no clock or whistle, but when Joe is calling plays we probably should. Nicknamed Payton for his love of intricate play calling, audibles and all, Joe is the human rain delay!

10. The ball is considered dead "when a backward pass or fumble by a player strikes the ground." So, the ball cannot be turned over on a fumble unless it pops up in the air and is caught before hitting turf. Also, play stops as soon as the ball carrier touches the ground with anything other than his speedy cleats.

11. "The offensive team is responsible for retrieving the ball after a down." When a bullet of a pass splits two receivers and skids thirty yards downfield, you've never seen people look so quickly in the opposite direction. I fear the whiplash! This almost as much as I fear having to be the one to go get the ball.

12. "Any player may hand the ball forward or backward at any time." Just know that in pickup pigskin, as soon as the ball leaves the quarterback's hands, the defense can rush. Also, you are allowed just one blitz per four downs.

13. "All players are eligible to touch or catch a pass." Sometimes, though, this is not so. If we have odd numbers, for example, the center on the team that has the extra player is ineligible.

14. We award one point for a touchdown and have no point-after attempts. However, the fun-loving folks at the U of F do something kind of interesting when it comes to extra points: "An opportunity to score one point from the three-yard line, two points from the ten-yard line, or three points from the twenty-yard line by running or passing shall be granted to the team scoring a touchdown." A safety is usually worth two points, but in our format we only award one-half point. This odd choice of scoring was established long before I started to

After taking the pitch, BVA can either run or throw the ball to Steve, the "eligible" center breaking toward the camera. The defensive lineman (not pictured) has decided to stay home, rather than rush right in and possibly fall prey to some form of trickery.

play, but I've yet to see it impact the outcome of a game. To be honest, we're not really playing for the score, anyway.

15. Our guys play a pretty clean game. We've got kids and mortgages after all. But just in case you've got some boneheads in your midst, you might want to consider the following list of conduct no-nos: No player shall contact an opponent who is on the ground, throw a runner to the ground, deliberately dive or run into a defensive player, and/or tackle the runner by grasping or encircling with the hands or arms. No wet willies, either!

NIRSA also provides rules for co-ed games, which can be a pretty good time. And really, anyone who thinks the only place a woman has in football is cheering along the sidelines or posing in beer ads is sadly mistaken. Even high school powder-puff games can be fierce, let alone these co-ed leagues. Fierce but fun!

1. "An offensive male runner cannot advance the ball across the line of scrimmage." In the interest of fair play, only a woman can run with the ball. In order for a man to advance the ball, it must be via the pass.

2. "During the offensive team's possession there may not be two consecutive legal forward pass completions from a male passer to a male receiver."

3. Bonus: "A touchdown involving a female receiver/runner crossing the goal line or throwing a legal forward pass is worth 9 points." You go, girl!

OK, here now is another quiz to make sure you know what you'll do in any circumstance, enabling you to avoid those "On the Spot" rules committee scenarios. I'm not cruel, so this time we'll use everyone's favorite form of assessment: True or False. The answers can be found in the footnote, but no cheating!

1. True or False: If you trip the guy as he's blitzing past you, the penalty is that he can kiss your wife at the New Year's Eve party. With his tongue.

2. True or False: If you're guarding a receiver and refuse to respect his pass interference call, no one will ever again agree to take in your mail when you go on vacation.

3. True or False: In two-hand touch, if you only get one hand on the ball carrier but claim to have gotten him with both, the Football Fairy will come to your room that night and transform you into Ray Lewis's tackling dummy.[14]

All right, I'll be nice and give you one last review in case you slept through my class. First and foremost, set your field up so that

---

[14] *Answers: True, true, true! Also, most organized leagues are flag football, so the phantom two-hand touch isn't a problem.*

Eric is the man in the middle; the required man over center. But his teammates are there, too, stacked for a blitz, or maybe just trying to "show" blitz. Oh, the strategy!

it makes sense. The more players you have, the wider the field should be. The older your players are, the shorter the field should be! Next, count three Mississippis before you rush—no crossing the line ahead of time.[15] As soon as the ball changes hands, via a handoff, pitch, or pass, the defense can come on over and it doesn't count as a blitz. Speaking of which, one defender *must* line up over center. He doesn't have to be the guy to count, nor does he have to be the guy to rush; there just has to be somebody matched up with the snapper.

For every turn with the ball, your team can gain just one first down. Subsequently, if the quarterback gets dropped for a loss behind the marker, be it a pylon or lacrosse goal, your team cannot earn *another* first down. Football is a physical sport, but don't touch the receiver once he's five yards downfield. At the same

---

[15] *The savvy/sneaky player will edge in while counting—call him on that.*

time, watch out for receivers setting picks on defenders. It's up to you how harshly you want to penalize this, but in the NFL they can't set picks at all. . . . And finally, there is a mercy rule, but it has everything to do with the beating your bodies have taken and very little to do with the score. If you're taking the time to read this book, I don't expect you're the type to call it a game just because you're down a couple of TDs, anyway!

4

The "Not Quite Ready for Canton Players": Maroons, Not Morons!

I was in the seventh grade when we moved from Marion Avenue to Orchard Road. Fortunately, we still lived in Mt. Kisco, which meant I could go to the same school and have the same coaches. It was from them that I learned all about the all-American triple play: football, basketball, and baseball. These guys planted the weekend warrior seed in me.

The Mt. Kisco Maroons coaching staff knew the Xs and Os of football, but more importantly they knew how to get the most out of their players. Whether it was with a gut check or a beer, they never wavered in their dedication. And they certainly never faltered when it came to keeping us in line. For example, we won the league championship in seventh grade and maybe got a little big for our britches. So, before the year-end party, they called for one last practice. The optimists thought it would be some sort of a reward, while the pessimists were sure we'd have to run one final set of suicides—for an hour and a half! The truth fell somewhere in between as head coach Bud Jobin said, "Your ball first." And then they lined up across from us, without equipment.

Seven of them versus eleven of us and, of course, we could sub when somebody got thumped. They couldn't. Then again, they never needed to. They did all of the thumping that day, reminding us that we weren't quite as tough as we thought we were. I'd gotten a little dose of modesty the summer before, too. The move to Orchard Road complete, there was some money left over for a family vacation. So, we all piled into the Nova and drove down to Foggy Bottom. Although it was July, ninety degrees, and humid, I kept my Maroons jacket on throughout. Such pride! We were at the Washington Zoo when some little kid pointed at the name on the back and asked his mother, "Mommy, what's a moron?"

It was instant family folklore, like the Big Bird nickname and the office Super Bowl pool. I was going to throw the kid to the lions, but instead with great indignation said, "Maroons. Not morons. Duh!" Yep, that's how I tried to dispel the notion that I was a moron. . . .

In my mind, in the collective mind of everybody on the team, we were the rawest, meanest, biggest, most championest group of seventh and eighth graders ever assembled on the field of play. With that overinflated image, we just couldn't understand how our coaches could be so confident in their durability and skills. How dare they play us without helmets and shoulder pads? No cleats? One guy even wore his work boots! To further add to our disbelief, they won—easily. Afterward, the seven of them walked off of the field, cracked open the cooler, and started cracking on us. We were down-and-out, as even worse than the defeat was the fact that football season was now over. I'm sure they felt the same.

A week later, I received an award at the team dinner. It came wrapped in Band-Aids and athletic tape. This, because my mother had insisted I wear a protective vest for my ribs, as well as a neck roll. The doctored trophy offended me much less than the kid at the zoo—this was back in the day when coaches could still rile up their players without worrying about causing debilitating illnesses like *crushedus self-esteemus*. This was when players wanted to work for the coach's respect rather than whine for it. And if they got a little too big for their britches, somebody would cut them down to size right quick. Nowadays, coaches have to answer—at length and ad nauseam—questions about playing time and play selection even if they've already explained into the merciless telephone that they're trying to eat dinner with the family. It's a shame. I really do think the world was a better place when the coaches were in control. I have no doubt that each of us, as individuals and as a team, was better off for it.

As further proof, in eighth grade I won the Coach's Award. No tape and no Band-Aids this time, just a nod to how hard I'd worked to improve. Of course, getting a Coach's Award is a backhanded compliment. It's like hearing that you're not the prettiest girl at the dance, but you sure are a nice conversationalist. Everybody wants to be the MVP. I wanted to be the MVP.[16] But I didn't question their judgment; I accepted it as the truth. I would've walked through fire for those guys, each and every one.

Putting the coaches of the Mt. Kisco Maroons into my "Not Quite Ready for Canton Players" Hall of Fame has little to do

---

[16] *I will admit that I never did exceed expectations in football. The taped-up trophy was more of a prophecy than the Coach's Award.*

with their love of the game; even less to do with the fact that they handed out trophies and occasionally shared the cooler with us. No, these coaches make The Hall because they dedicated so much of their time to teaching us—teaching us in the manner of their choosing, take it or leave it. A lot of weekend warriors are coaches, and although putting up with parent complaints is a job hazard, far worse is the fact that nobody dares take a risk these days. The legal ramifications are just too great, so rare is the time you will see a player benched for attitude, a coach cutting on a kid to keep him on his toes, or a coach and player sharing a celebratory pop. *The Bad News Bears* looks like over-the-top fiction when Buttermaker hands his boys a beer after their run at the championship, but this used to be the reality. Our coaches had a tradition of not only throwing a keg party at the end of the season, but also having a beer with us in the back of the bus. It was one of those rites of manhood that all young jocks (i.e., future weekend warriors) should be able to enjoy. Like watching your younger brother cop a feel off of Danette Partellow as the varsity quarterback looks on with jealousy!

After road games, the coaches called each of the starters to the back of the bus, one at a time, to discuss performance. Usually, I'd hear one crack, one compliment, three or four strongly worded suggestions, and then a "Good game. Now get lost." There was a smile on my face, for sure, as I walked back to my seat. By the way, it was one beer and it was a light beer, so shelve those concerns of child abuse. Besides, what are you going to do? Call the cops? The police chief's son was our defensive backs coach!

I know now why these coaches cared to not only play with us, but to also spend all of that time coaching. They were weekend warriors, and weekend warriors will do whatever they can to be on the field of play; to feel the heat of competition before, during, and after the coin toss; to invite the aches and pains of an equip-ment-less game as a trade-off for sixty more minutes of fun, no matter how moronic that may seem.

And the inductees are . . .
the coaches of the Mt. Kisco Maroons,
for all their dedication, winning ways,
trophies, and Lite beer from Miller.

5

You Got Gear

EQUIPPING YOURSELF

Let's get one thing straight: I don't subscribe to the theory that the clothes make the man. It's more like the clothing manufacturer makes the money! Nike and company might produce inspiring ads, but when it comes to a fifteen-degree morning, I'm more likely to turn to L.L. Bean and Orvis than the swoosh.

I may not be into the newest gear, but I am into sandwiches. Mmmm, sandwiches! Whether or not you like a nice roast beef, cheddar, and Thousand Island on a hard roll, make sure to buy yourself some sandwich bags.[17] Thus begins the advice-giving that is the "You Got Gear" chapter.

As tough as it can be to play in the cold, it can be far worse, far more miserable, and—with the possibility of torn tendons, the

---

[17] *Seriously, just one or two spoonfuls of Thousand Island dressing and I'm running the forty in four-flat. It does wonders for the sandwich, too.*

flu, and pneumonia—far more costly in the co-pay department to play wet. So in order to keep your feet dry, get some sandwich bags the next time you're at the grocery store. Then, before slipping your cleats over your socks, put one on each foot. Maybe even two.

The sandwich bags will act as both insulator and waterproofing system. Although it's not 100 percent foolproof, it's the only thing you can do when running through puddles and dodging raindrops. Push the aluminum foil to one side, the wax paper to the other, and reach for those bags, friend. You won't regret it.

So, starting from the roots up, you've got socks and sandwich bags, and over these you're going to wear cleats. Running on a field—grass or turf—is tremendously stressful on your lower half, and cleats will offset some of that stress. In particular, they will help you to save your groin. (Do you need any more motivation than that?!) You probably won't realize it while playing, but all

Use some electrical tape for the heel and use a sandwich bag to keep the feet dry. A pair of waterproof pants will help, too.

the cutting—left then right to tail your man, right then left to try and get open in the end zone—takes a toll on your groin. It's like the axle or fulcrum or whatever that mechanical word is. Everything swivels from your crotch, and if you slip even just a little bit while running, it's this precious region that will bear the brunt. Give yourself some footing and you'll minimize the ache. You'll also be a mess on coverage if you can't keep up with your man. He'll blow right by you, and before you know it you'll have a nickname: "Toast"—because you've been burned! Save the tennis shoes for tennis.

On to the knees. If you have even an inkling of a problem, go to the store and get yourself some knee support. Not only will it lengthen your career, it looks kind of tough to be all strapped up like that, like something out of *Mad Max*. Yes, indeed, you *can* be an intimidator with your gear!

If it's cold, no one will see your brace because you'll be wearing pants. And if it's raining you'll want to wear waterproof pants. I play with a couple of fishermen, so they have appropriate all-weather gear. I do not fish and I do not have appropriate all-weather gear. Next year, I'll surely pick some up, though. This is what I tell myself every year as I suffer through yet another bout of bubonic plague (my doctor calls this a sinus infection, the joker). The kids I teach can't bring me down with their germs, but an hour and a half of February football and I'm a mess.[18]

Whether it's wind pants or shorts, I wear spandex underneath just to keep everything from flopping around. There's enough to worry about when your guy breaks right and you've got to cross over to keep up without having to also concern yourself with crushing the ol' baby makers between your thighs . . . Half of the guys I play with have had their tubes tied and still they wear

---

[18] *Is it still worth it? You bet.*

spandex. It might have seemed unmanly when we were growing up, but sometimes even us weekend warriors have to succumb to common sense. Fashion de rigueur, too!

On that note, I wear a cup in softball, but not in football. It just isn't necessary. (It's tough to type with your fingers crossed, but that's exactly how I wrote that last sentence. Veeeeery superstitious . . .) Most of our hard-core contact comes north of the belly button and, thankfully, not in the danger zone below.

OK, enough talk about the groin. Staying up top, a waterproof top is also recommended, especially because the more soaked your clothing gets, the slower you will be. One day this past winter, it rained, and within five minutes, I'd gained ten pounds in water weight. It's hard enough to get open on a post pattern without adding on those pounds. Find a sweatshirt/jacket/scuba suit and wear it. And while on that rainy- day note, a hat to keep the rain out of your face will be a big help. If it's snowing, warmth is the priority, but if it's rain you're worrying about, put something with a brim on.

I wear a baseball cap and although it gets soaked, I'm able to pick the quarterback out between the raindrops without fear of Old Man River running into my eyes. In the cold weather months, I go with a wool hat. And in both weather scenarios, I wear rubberized gloves. They keep my hands dry and provide some grip to help catch the ball. They're tight enough that I've even been able to wear them while playing quarterback. I shouldn't attempt throws of more than twenty yards on a perfect day, let alone during inclement weather, but with those gloves on, ten- to fifteen-yard routes are well within reason. I found them in the outdoors section at Wal-Mart, so maybe there is hope for me as a fisherman.[19]

---

[19] *If I keep this up,* Fishing for Weekend Warriors *will be next!*

BVA got himself a pair, too. And so now it's time for a gratuitous ZZ Top sing-along: "He's got gloooooves, and he knows how to use them."

There is also the issue of dental bills. These can be killer, as even those of us fortunate enough to have decent dental plans pay through the nose (or mouth, if you like that kind of humor) whenever we go. So, it might not be a bad idea to wear a mouthguard. Mike sports one now, so as to avoid rechipping his tooth, and even though it makes it a little more inconvenient to breathe, he's yet to pass out on us. An added bonus is the feeling of nostalgia you'll get as you boil some water to set the mold.

Before moving on, I will also discuss electrical tape. I suggest picking up a roll if you're going to be a weekend warrior. (Besides, what workbench is complete without a roll of electrical tape?) First and foremost, you can seal your sleeves closed at the wrist,

Wrap up that wrist—not for protection from injury, but to save yourself from the aggravation of the sneaky snow.

which helps to keep the snow from sneaking up your arms. And economically speaking, if you don't feel like shelling out fifty dollars for another pair of cleats, electrical tape can keep a pair of "go fasters" going for another year, at least. Holes and torn heels are no match for a couple of crisscrosses of electrical tape. And if you think those knee braces are intimidating, just wait until you settle in at the line, a blitz still at your discretion and electrical tape covering you from head to toe. Mucho macho.

EQUIPPING THE FIELD

In basketball you bring the ball and only the ball because the hoops are already there. The same goes for softball. There's a fence or there isn't a fence. In football, though, you need the proper gear to have the best possible game. And as you'll want to create the best possible field, prepare to steal some pylons!!!

Or buy some. Go to any place that sells soccer equipment and they'll have the small orange kind. Talk to a friend who works for the highway department and you'll get the bigger ones, which are

Outside of the football, pretty much all you need is a bag of jerseys and pylons to mark the goal line. If we had two more, we'd be sure to mark the back of the end zone, as well.

preferable. Just be sure to get at least six of them; ten, if possible. Two of the pylons will mark off the halfway point; the proverbial line in the sand. The halfway point is, to state the obvious, the forty-yard line if you play on the typical eighty-yard field; the fifty-yard line if you're nuts. The other four pylons are used to mark the end zones. If you only have four more, you will obviously mark the two goal lines, but if you've got eight, you can do the back lines, too. This is pretty important for those corner-of-the-end-zone, jump-ball kinds of routes. The receiver certainly can't watch his feet while he's focusing on the ball, and the defender better not be looking down. It's just a lot easier to judge touchdown or no touchdown if you have pylons in back.

Even if you're able to play on a lined gridiron, use the pylons. They really stand out and their visibility makes the game that much more exciting. The receivers know exactly where to cut off their routes, and the defensive backs are well aware of what they can give and what they cannot. The scrambling quarterback also knows where to pull up short if he's managed to find some open field. Why cross the first down marker when you can give yourself one or two shots downfield before "settling" for the first (which is only a yard away)? Any quarterback who knows their stuff will run out of bounds right before the orange pylon at midfield. When you've got second and short, the play-calling options are endless.

And now, what would a chapter on gear be without mentioning a football? My pigskin advice is this: It doesn't matter if you're playing with a pro ball (long live "The Duke"), a college ball, or an animal bladder, just let a little bit of air out of it—makes it easier for the quarterback to grip and throw and a little bit easier for the receiver to hold onto. You'll notice that this happens naturally in the cold-weather months, anyway, if you leave the ball in

Although Dr. John is putting his team in position to get the first, the point of this photo is to show you the pylons for the first down and end zone. We had three-on-three that day, so it was a sixty-yard field.

your trunk. Just don't let it get *too* flat; otherwise, you and your boys will be flinging around a Frisbee!

Another piece of equipment that will add miles of enjoyment to the games is the pinny. I know, I know, pinnies are what you wore back in the days of gym class. But really, you're going to want to know who's on your team and who isn't.[20] Obviously, if you're playing two-on-two in the street, pinnies aren't necessary. But anything more than two-on-two and your quarterback is going to need to be able to tell who's on his team, who's getting open, and who's closing in for the INT. Paul, our patron saint of pigskin, has a couple of old white jerseys and they do the trick. If you're just starting out, though, and don't have white jerseys, pick up a couple of pinnies. I did an Internet search that took me all of five seconds and found a dozen orange nylon (and nylon rhymes with pylon!) pinnies for forty-five dollars. You can probably find a better deal than that, though.

And just for a little historical insight, you don't need to feel weird wearing your pinny, as they've been around since before rugby and soccer got divorced. Originally referred to as pinafores, they were worn by kids to keep their clothes clean while eating. Sloppy kids and weekend warrior football players—oh, the similarities!

Here's one last piece of equipment advice: Bring a water bottle. Unlike some of the other favorite weekend warrior sports, there probably won't be any beverages around—at least not the kind that help rehydrate old guys like us. So remember to take a break and drink some water. Taking a water break allows you to take a break from running up and down the field. And isn't that a break we could all use?

---

[20] *And shirts versus skins just isn't a good idea anymore. With each passing year, we move further away from the days when a six-pack was a physical feature and not just a postgame staple.*

6

The "Not Quite Ready for Canton Players": Puddles, Pulling Guards, and the Polar Bear Club

After the drills and thrills of the Maroons, freshman football practice was pretty tame. It was also pretty friggin' unorganized, as the coach was an old guidance counselor who only took the job to pad his pre-retirement salary. When we asked him about defensive schemes, "Coach" Gilmore told us to "chase the guy with the ball." Needless to say, even after practice we were ready to play. We wanted more!

It might be that Coach Gilmore went easy on us, or maybe it's just that thirteen-year-old boys never get tired.[21] Either way,

---

[21] *This also goes for a couple of thirty-something weekend warriors I know. Some guys just have no quit in them, and to these men of endless energy I raise my glass (while sitting down).*

four of us decided one night to skip the post-pizza dessert and go play. Not only had we just finished practice, the next day we had a game, but what did we care? As the temperature dipped below fifty for the first time since March, we set off for some "Puddles and Pulling Guards." What concrete and curb had been to family football, this game was to us freshmen.

In the new neighborhood, we'd traded Dave and Danette in for a rock star. Rick Wills, the bass player for Foreigner, lived at the end of the road, and rather than drinking and drugging he did things like maintain the town land we all called Haynes Field. Wiffle Ball in the spring and summer, football in the fall and winter. "Puddles and Pulling Guards" after it rained.

Basically, the way to play is you pick the biggest puddle and make that the point of contact. The puddle never moves, so the line of scrimmage never moves. This is where the pulling guard meets the defensive lineman and where, if the linebacker is doing his job, the ball carrier goes down in a spray of water, mud, and muck, four arms wrapped around his legs! There is no passing and there are no first downs. Two guys on offense, two guys on defense. One puddle, one football. Beautiful in its simplicity and simple in its beauticity. Whatever all that means. It was down-and-dirty football, and we couldn't get enough—until Darrell bonked his head on a rock hidden somewhere below the surface of the line of scrimmage and couldn't remember what Coach Gilmore's defensive scheme was.

With fading sunlight and bloody brow, we decided it was time to head home. Passing Rick Wills's house, Darrell sang "You're as cold as ice!" which was almost as clever as his observation: "You know, we're just like that Flying Eskimos Club. With jumping in the puddle and all."

It took a minute before James could interpret. "Do you mean the Polar Bear Club, jackass?"

"Oh yeah."

You just can't find fun like this after a croquet match. Brain damage, neither.

I don't remember if we won the game the following day, but that was football the way I liked it; the way I like it still. Down and dirty, with leftover pizza as a part of the postgame routine. And it's worth noting that the happiest I ever saw Rick Wills was not on stage at the Nassau Coliseum, jamming out to "Cold As Ice." That was happy, sure, but his happiest moments were on his ride-on mower, trimming Haynes Field for us. He was such a regular guy. You could just tell he'd be out playing "Puddles and Pulling Guards" if not for the upcoming tour, etc., etc.[22] That's the crappy side of adulthood: There's never a good time to risk a broken collarbone in the name of fun. When is it acceptable for a grown man to tackle a friend in a puddle? How about Saturday morning at a quarter after eight?

And the inductees are . . .
Rick Wills (for mowing) and my mother (for hosing us down when we got home). Darrell, too, for giving my rotisserie teams a name: Viva los Flying Eskimos!!!

---

[22] *Or, more likely, rugby, as he was a boot-drinking Brit.*

7

"I Swear,
I Won't Get Hurt!"

Nobody in the world cares for us like our mothers . . . except our wives. And this makes these women formidable opponents. Mothers should be appreciated, but wives must be handled with care. From the other end of the phone, your mother cannot put a stop to your athletic antics. But the wife . . . the wife is another story! Our better halves want us safe and sound, home, and definitely not at play. Thus, the need for you to cover up the aches and pains.

In the other *Weekend Warrior* books, the recommendations I made pertaining to the little white lie had everything to do with getting out of the house for fun and very little to do with hiding injury. But in order to be a pigskin-playing weekend warrior, there will be many a morning that you have to outwit, outmaneuver, or even outright defy Nurse Nuptials. Just know that the punishment is double when you do get hurt. You can just forget about the ice and Advil room service. At least for an hour or so; but then, sure

Al and Mike clear the field, making sure the lacrosse goal is far enough out of bounds so as to avoid injury.

as the sun also rises, her maternal instinct will kick in and she'll come to your rescue just like long ago, when Mama made soup.[23]

And yes, you will whine to her. I know it because you, like me, do a pretty good job of holding it in while around the fellas. So much so that we can't help but turn into crybabies once we get home. We need an outlet, and those soft hands and sympathetic eyes are oh-so-tempting. But the same way you must be frugal with the fabrications, don't go overboard with the complaining. Otherwise, you'll never get out again. She *will* quote you. And using our words against us is one of their oldest tricks, gents. Consider yourselves warned!

You may get the attention and affection you so desire, but there will come a time when you want out. Inevitably, a quarter to eight on Saturday morning will roll around and you'll picture your boys,

[23] *Plus, deep down inside, she loves the fact that you still act like a little boy sometimes. What's more attractive—the slob on the couch with the remote glued to his hand, or the muddied man who likes to run and have fun?*

scattered all around town in their various kitchens, mudrooms, and garages, gulping down coffee while slipping on their sandwich bags and sweats. You'll feel the leather in your hands, the turf beneath your toes, and the call of the wild. Miracle of miracles, the ache in your back has subsided, the twang in your groin is twanging no more, and that sore Achilles feels a hundred times better. You'll wonder what all your bitching was about. The moaning, too. Flat on your back for the past two days, all you could do was look up at the ceiling, but now, now all you can see is downfield; that pylon in the corner of the end zone. All you can hear is the quarterback detailing the play and then the celebration when it works out as planned. That is, until she snaps you out of your reverie by repeating the question that you just subconsciously ignored.

"Are you suuuure you should play today?"

The fact that she has a point, the fact that her question has an obvious answer—an obvious answer for you *and* an obvious, albeit different, answer for her—well, it makes us fight even harder for what we so deep-down-desperately want.

"Yeah. I'm sure. I've got at least one more trip up and down left in this old body!"

"Well, you know, I was talking to . . . " and at this point she launches into a story about a friend's husband, a guy still laid up in bed a week after playing Parcheesi with his kids; something about him reaching to move a game piece and hearing a crack in his back. In her mind, it's a reasonable comparison: these are the things that happen to people. She just doesn't understand that you'll deal with it *when* it happens to you and not *before* it happens to you.

And so, my friend, you must do all you can to cut the umbilical cord.

Besides, a lie for exercise's sake is more than justifiable. It's near expected! For once in your life, you're not looking to drink sour mash with the boys. You're not desperate to get to the strip club for that bachelor party. This lie isn't about a gambling debt or a salacious credit card charge. You are confident because you have the best of intentions. You simply want to play.

Men are genetically programmed to make excuses; the ability to fib comes from our chromosomal makeup, or something like that. So, even if you're out of practice, fear not. It's merely a matter of reawakening your sleeping DNA. Deep down inside, you have a Rolodex of excuses that has been sitting dormant since the glory days. There's no lock on that Rolodex, brother. Dust it off and open 'er up!

But if you're still not sure, then feel free to borrow from me. Whichever excuse you choose, tailor it to your needs, and best of luck.

TOP FIVE EXCUSES FOR PLAYING

5. Channeling Tony the Tiger to be both convincing and humorous, you say: "No need to worry. I feel greeeeat!"

4. "Without me they'll have odd numbers and odd numbers means an ineligible center. You don't want me to be responsible for an ineligible center, do you?"

3. "Next year I turn [fill in the blank], you know. Who knows how much longer I'll be able to play?" Work that sympathy rap.

2. "But Al has that Tupperware thingy his wife borrowed from you and he said he'd bring it today."

1. "I feel fat. Do I look fat?"

If that last line can't get you out the door, nothing will. Wish your buddies well, become the poster child for Chubby Hubby ice cream, and prepare for a life of armchair quarterbacking. It's over.

All kidding aside, let's say you are legitimately hurting. If you're like me, that L5S1 tends to kick up its heels every now and again, bucking like a bronco and sending you to the orthopedist for a pill (hopefully not Vioxx or Celebrex) and to the heating pad for some serious R and R. Better to miss a week than a month, so it's now time to lie to yourself:

TOP FIVE EXCUSES FOR PLAYING NEXT TIME

5. "I've been meaning to organize the desktop on my computer."
4. "Sure, hon, banana pancakes sound great! I'll just play next week." You're a finished man when pancakes become the priority.
3. "I can't find my lucky T-shirt and there's no way I can play without my lucky T-shirt. All righty then, I guess I'm not going . . ."
2. "I think I'll watch cartoons with the kids instead." Piss-poor excuse, especially given the fact that there is no longer anything on par with *Justice League, Scooby-Doo, Fat Albert,* or *Schoolhouse Rock.* At least you'll retain your Good Dad status with the wife and kids.
1. "I don't like football that much anyway." Your nose is growing, Pinocchio. On the bright side, you won't have to ask Nurse Geppetto to tie your shoelaces in the morning.

Before we move on, a list of bonus excuses to use on your boys when you can't make it due to the wife, the boss, the kids, friends coming into town, or an injury.

TOP FIVE BONUS EXCUSES TO GIVE THE GUYS FOR PLAYING NEXT TIME

1. I can't make it because of the wife.
2. I can't make it because of the boss.

3. I can't make it because of the kids.

4. I can't make it because of friends coming into town.

5. I can't make it because I don't like you.[24]

In other words, to be a pigskin-playing weekend warrior you'll probably have to lie on occasion—not to free yourself up from responsibility, but about the condition of your decrepit body. And you'd better work out the kinks now because the older you get, the more you'll have to lie. And the more you lie, the better you'll have to be at it. It's a vicious cycle, but with a pot o' gold and six points at the end of the rainbow.

It was not a nagging wife that Eric (right) had to overcome, but losing his big toe in a fight with the lawn mower. After surgery he spent a couple of months on the DL, but was back in fine form by October.

---

[24] *It's better to say anything than to use an injury as an excuse. Even if it's a legitimate excuse!*

8

The "Not Quite Ready for Canton Players": When the Time Has Come . . .

I knew that it was time to hang 'em up when pregame became painful.

It was the night of the big bowl championship; Section I of the New York State Public School Athletic League. It was huge. (I'm not being sarcastic. It doesn't get any bigger than this in the Northeast!) The Fox Lane Foxes versus the White Plains Tigers. And yes, I was a Fox.

As a junior and senior, we won both of our bowl games. For a smaller school it was an uncanny dominance that grew out of those formative years with the Maroons. I was on the team for the first one, but not for the second. I do love football, but the writing was on the wall. Although I'd once been much bigger than 99 percent of the other players, they'd all caught up to me. It also didn't help that 99 percent of these other players could now bench more than me! The final straw came during warm-ups for that first bowl game. I was banging shoulder pads with Kevin—hands crossed in front and each of us pulling toward one another with the force of rams—when I became aware of how much it was making my shoulder hurt.[25] And once you start to feel pain, once you start to even think about pain, especially during calisthenics, your football career is over.

Going into senior year, I was number one on the depth chart at defensive end, punter, and kicker, but just couldn't get up for double sessions when August rolled around. Instead, I went to a couple of Grateful Dead shows, hung out at the town pool with my buddies, and made plans to do something the night of Homecoming other than be home before curfew. The time had come . . . I was now an official weekend warrior.

I should have seen the signs. The night before the bowl game I couldn't sleep and rather than watch a movie to pump me up (something like *Red Dawn* or *Rambo* or *The Longest Yard*) I made a T-shirt. It included Coach Mezaros's rally cry, "Battlogize," and other such team-uniting mottos. A fox head or two, too.

And just so that I never forget what a dork I'd become, there is a newspaper photo featuring the team in a big celebratory pile-up, including me out of my jersey and shoulder pads—not that they did me any good anyway!—and in that homemade T-shirt. Leave it to the kicker . . .

---

[25] *I almost said "Ouch," but caught myself, fortunately.*

And the inductees are . . .
Kevin, for knocking some sense into me, and CJ, for leading us to those two bowl wins. He was the only quarterback I've ever seen who could smile his way around a defensive end.

9

Gluteus Maximus and Other Muscles Just Waitin' to Be Pulled

A s a thirty-four-year-old, there is no greater victory, no better "trophy," than to hear that you are "Preferred Plus."

I was recently awarded this status. That's right, sports fans, I am unbelievably, inexplicably, "Preferred Plus!" For those of you who have yet to pee in a cup in the comfort of your own home, when you get life insurance a nurse comes to the house, takes some blood, sends you into the commode, and even has the nerve to ask you to step up onto a scale. It's eight o'clock at night, you haven't eaten since lunch—one of many efforts you've made to ensure "Preferred Plus"—and now you must suffer the indignity of getting weighed. In front of your wife.

But if you're getting out to play football on a regular basis, you stand a fighting chance. Trust me when I tell you, I was shocked to learn that I was going to get the best possible rate on my life insurance. I am not the picture of health, but a month after ushering the nurse out of my house as quick as you can whisper, "Put that pizza into the oven, hon!" I got this great, money-saving news. Let it be the incentive now for you to read this chapter.

In his book, *Swimming for Fitness*, Kelvin Juba writes: "It is common knowledge now that you should warm up the body before undertaking any form of exercise. This has the effect of preparing the heart, muscles, and joints." And if you need to do these kinds of things for swimming, it should be obvious what kind of warming up football requires. Especially when talking about guys who spend five days a week sitting at a desk and the other two in front of the television!

Simply put, warming up increases the temperature of the muscles so that they can contract and relax more quickly. It also raises—gradually rather than suddenly and traumatically—the

After putting the first-down marker into place, Al is ready to get loose. There's plenty of time for warming up as teams are chosen, pinnies distributed, and the field laid out.

heart rate, loosens the connective tissue, and triggers the release of fluid that promotes the smooth movement of bone over bone. The older we get, the less smooth we become. The only fluid we get is on the knee. Without stretching there can be no fluidity, and without fluidity there can be no extra effort. There are certainly times when I take it easy on a play, but I always feel guilty as I'm doing it. I feel like I'm letting my team down. I know it might sound silly to some, but if you have that competitive spirit, then you know exactly what I mean. You should always be loose enough, sharp enough, in shape enough to play where your team needs you. It is the mission of all athletes from pros to high schoolers to old men in old cleats to put their team in the best position to win. Your boys should never have to make a sacrifice because you're winded.

And you will get winded. Running in thirty-four-degree weather at thirty-four years of age just ain't the same as running in eighty-degree weather at eighteen. You'd breathe deep except that your lungs, despite being surrounded by a warming wall of fat, can't expand because they're frozen! You know you should be standing upright with your hands above your head, but it's all you can do to keep from falling over. So the compromise is, you bend over, heaving for breath, and pray that the quarterback tells you to run the little, distractionary three-yard down and out.

I'd have to say that the last time I was in good (meaning *good*) shape was when I was twenty-four.[26] I had a health club membership, ran full full-court basketball like it was reading the *Sunday Times*, and could only afford soup for dinner and cereal for breakfast. (Lunch hadn't yet been invented.) In the interceding years, I've finally started earning salary enough to eat, I gave up the membership in lieu of procreating, and I herniated a disc.

---

[26] *Can that really be ten years ago?*

This meant the end of true full-court basketball and the beginning of my life as a guy who stretches.

It was Columbus Day when my roommate James and I went to play a nice little game of racquetball. I haven't seen that guy since. And by this I mean me, not James! It took me two years to recover to the point where I could play softball, full-court hoops (the short way), and two-hand touch. But even now, there is a condition: I have to condition myself, starting with the back. There is the stretching, but there is also the bedtime routine. I read at night, for at least a half an hour, with the heating pad on my lower back. I do this every night. (I even bring the heating pad with me on road trips.) I also avoid sleeping on my stomach, which was always my most comfortable position, as this is guaranteed to lock me up the following day. Speaking of the following day, every morning I shave in the shower. Bending over the sink just kills my lower back, so now I am a shower shaver. And the headline reads: Shower Shaver Saves His Back! Say that ten times fast.

I know I can't get out to play if my body parts keep breaking down, but this doesn't mean that I've turned into Richard Simmons either. Despite my status as "Preferred Plus" (you should have seen the rekindled glow of amour in the wife's eyes!), I'm still fond of drinking beer. Eating everything and anything that comes with melted cheese too, which leads me to my real weakness, in terms of *not* being the picture of health and *not* doing all the right exercises. Welcome to the portion of the show entitled "Do As I Say, Not as I Do."

The first thing a doctor will tell you when discussing your newly acquired bad back is to work on strengthening your stomach. The muscles of your stomach work hand in hand with the muscles of your back, after all. I used to do tons of sit-ups, but it just bothers my back too much now. When you herniate a L5S1, you become like a piece of cardboard about to be ripped in two. It's as if the weekend warrior gods are preparing the recycling bin and just can't fit that pizza box in. They bend it forward then back, forward then back, loosening the compressed material until it is weak enough to break. On the bad days, that's exactly how my back feels. Yours, too, I'm sure. But if you can do the sit-ups, do them. You may feel like you're preparing yourself to be taken out with the trash, but it'll be worth it. If only I could follow my own advice!

Even if I bail on the sit-up thing, there's plenty of other advice I'm willing and able to follow. For one, I can stretch. And stretch I do when it comes to my back, legs, and groin. In all of the other weekend warrior books, players are advised to stretch at the rink, field, court, or course. This is not always the case for football. Due to the weather, there will be plenty of times when you're forced to risk the elements at home. In my case, the dog and daughter . . .

Nutsy, as you will soon see, helps Joe with his groin, while Noelle lends me a hand at home. Matty, too.

What was once the bench press is now the baby press!

On decent days, though, it's best to stretch out at the field, right before the game starts. The following pregame ritual, presented in photo essay format, should be altered depending on injuries, personal preference, and how wet the ground is! No matter how or where, just be sure to stretch, stretch, stretch.

Joe gets his groin stretched . . . Now that's man love! I recommend doing this thrice and holding it for at least five seconds each time.

This stretch is good for everything from hips to hammies, mobility to the receding hairline.

The hurdler stretch: as useful today as it was in your teens, if not more. Now touch those toes, Joe!

From hurdling to hiking, this is the mountain climber, good for the soul and good for the hammies. And remember, any stretch that helps your hamstrings will help your back.

See? Giants and Jets fans can get along!

And let's not forget that in this fast-paced world of over-booked Palm Pilots, diaper changes, work deadlines, dating ulti-matums, and whatever else is crowding your day, sometimes the best thing for the body is to just stop for a minute . . . relax . . . feel the terra firma beneath your body . . . and see the blue sky up above. Breathe easy.

And in this spirit . . . behold the "All-Over Body Stretch."

I'd say the All-Over Body Stretch is officially all over! Nutsy sure does miss tackle football . . .

My postgame ritual lasts the rest of the day. Not to say that it's all I do the rest of the day, not at all—not with the penance to pay for having two hours of playtime—but I'm sure to stretch a bit while the shower warms up, at least once more in the afternoon, and again before getting into bed. I don't care if it's after midnight, I still go through my nighttime routine. First, I put two pillows under the sheets, near the foot of the bed, and then I get that heating pad warmed up. About fifteen minutes into my book, I move the heating pad a little to get my upper back. Fifteen minutes later, it's lights out. I throw the heating pad to the floor (remembering to turn it off, of course), as well as one of the pillows, but keep the other pillow in bed with me for the night. I sleep on my side, with the pillow between my knees so that my back will feel like a million bucks come morning. Well, maybe ten bucks . . .

I know what you're doing right now: the same thing you do as the doctor tells you to do more of this and less of that. You're tuned in, your head nodding agreeably, but as soon as you put this

Pillow for head, heating pad for lower back, and two pillows for under the knees. Bushel of kale on the night table, too (stay tuned . . .).

book down you're going to go back to all of your old habits—your bad habits.

Big mistake.

Football is a physical game, and if you're not physically fit you won't be able to play. It isn't just torn tendons that can put you on the DL. The slightest strain of the groin and you're gone. A hamstring unstrung, a back as bad as Grampa's, a crick in the neck, an arm that you can't raise above your shoulder for no apparent reason—all of these things can keep you from your duties as a split end. The worst part may be having to miss a couple of months, but it's no holiday having to explain yourself to Nurse Nuptials either. To crawl across the bedroom floor begging for morphine is demoralizing. To have to ask for help pulling on your pants is also a real dent in the ego. Nothing screams "Old bastard!" like whining to the wife about a strained love handle or pizza box back.

People at work will be twice as cruel. You see, your injury doesn't really affect them. You can't beg out of a meeting because your groin is grumpy or you've got a bum back.[27] You're going to have to walk into the room, all eyes upon you, and there's sure to be at least one comment about the hitch in your gitch.

I am considered obese by the whatchamacallit standards, thus the shock over being deemed "Preferred Plus." I weigh 215 pounds and pop ten milligrams of Lipitor every day. I have a deep-seated weakness for baked goods and beer, so I called upon some knowledgeable folks to better explain all of this to all of us. For starters, in their book *Take Care of Yourself*, Donald Vickery and James Fries (Mmmmmm . . . French fries . . .) make some recommendations. And I, the picture of health, couldn't agree with them more.

---

[27] *That being said, something like three hundred thousand million work hours are missed every year due to bad backs. It just ain't good for the Gross National Product.*

For one, have your blood pressure checked every year. Make sure the ol' ticker doesn't rev too high when hauling ass in man-to-man coverage. It's also important that your heart be able to return to resting rate as quickly as possible. For more on this, talk to someone who didn't get a 67 percent in biology. I do know that bad cholesterol is bad while good cholesterol is good, so listen to me in regard to cholesterol testing. Although that French fries health guy thinks that going every five years is fine, I say you go every year. That's right. Once a year, down to the strip mall vampire. It'll take fifteen minutes, give or take, and then you'll be in the know. And I have come up with a simple give-and-take mathematical formula to convince you. As with all good formulas, beer is involved, so take heed.

According to my formula, as soon as you're legal to drink you need some sort of complimentary strategy for your annual physical. (And yes, I do recommend that you get a physical every year.) You may recall that once you turned twenty-one—back when dinosaurs ruled the earth and reality TV revolved around eat or be eaten—the good doctor started asking about your habits. Specifically, your smoking ("No, doc. Never!") and your drinking ("Sure, I have a beer or two a week."). Well, if you're going to—in the midst of this little white lie—divide by five the average number of beers you drink in a week, you'd be wise to also divide by five the amount of time you let pass between cholesterol counts.[28]

Beer formula or no beer formula, there are three types of people who *must* get tested on an annual basis: 1) those with an unusually high level of bad cholesterol, 2) those with a family history of high cholesterol, heart attacks, hypertension, etc., and 3) those John Candy disciples who can polish off the 96'er, gristle and all.[29]

---

[28] *I also got a 67 percent in math.*
[29] *See* The Great Outdoors *if you don't get this reference. You won't regret it!*

Get your cholesterol counted once a year and I may even cut you some slack with that other naughty C word: carbohydrates.

"Carbs are to your body what gas is to a car," writes Susan Kleiner in her book *High-Performance Nutrition*. "The major role of carbohydrates in nutrition is to provide energy. During exercise, carbohydrates are one of your main sources of energy."

And why is this energy so necessary? To be able to go from bed to breakfast to the end zone, you'll need to be gassed up. Gas up with proteins *and* carbs. Don't overdo it, especially right before leaving the house, but eat a healthy, well-balanced meal: a little of this, a little of that, maybe even some fruit, because if you have any designs on running crisp routes and playing tough D, you'll need to not only keep the weight down, you'll need to fight myoatrophy. My oh my, it's myoatrophy . . . Myoatrophy means that, between the ages of twenty and seventy, you will most likely lose up to 20 percent of your muscle mass. The change is more dramatic in men than in women, and this is true for even the healthiest of people. By eating right and staying physically active, especially if you maintain a routine of strength training, you can minimize the effects of myoatrophy. There are so many reasons to stay active—from contributing on the field to living longer to staying strong throughout that long life—that it's odd how often people need to be reminded. But we all forget. We are all swayed by the great movie on TNT; that Carvel ice cream cake; buffalo wings by the dozen. Eat three or four wings, but skip the cake and the movie. Go for a long walk. Throw the ball with your daughter, nephew, neighbor, whoever. Power up with a healthy diet that includes, yes, INCLUDES, carbs.

Keep in mind, though, there are carbs and then there are calories. Everybody agrees that controlling your caloric intake is a pretty good idea. To be specific, it's important to remember that as you lose muscle, your metabolic rate slows down, which means you will not burn calories as quickly as you once did.[30] We run like rabbits as kids. We trudge like turtles as adults. Obesity is a real threat, and being overweight often leads not to "Preferred Plus" but to heart disease, high blood pressure, diabetes, and other diabolic diseases. Diabetes is now one of the leading causes of death in the United States. As we get older, our bodies lose the ability to regulate glucose, and this can lead to adult onset, or Type II, diabetes. It's tough to rush the passer when they're amputating your foot.

Kleiner writes, "Maintaining muscle tissue helps normalize the flow of glucose from the blood into muscle cells where it can be properly used for energy."

Maintain your muscle mass and don't OD on the sugar. Keep in mind that one of the reasons so many kids are overweight these days is because fruit juice has just as much sugar as soda. The fast food doesn't help much either. As a teacher, I'm concerned with this epidemic of obese children. It might be fine and dandy to be a fatass when your surprise thirtieth birthday party is a thing of the not-so-recent past, but to see some of these chunky ten-year-olds waddling toward the cafeteria, it breaks my heart. (The Maroons' coaches would have to construct a fat boy trophy!) Seriously, these kids need to be outside playing with reckless abandon, not inside risking carpal tunnel and diabetes just so that they can get to the next level of a stupid video game.[31]

In addition to maintaining muscle and balancing proteins and carbs, think fiber. Not only will eating foods rich in fiber make you regular (yee ha!), these foods are necessary to avoid the plague. All right, not the plague, but the following ailments: appendicitis, cardiovascular disease, colorectal cancer, constipation (ugh), cavities and gum disease, erectile dysfunction (hoofa!),

---

[30] *Your back is the pizza box; your belly, the pizza. Buh-bye metabolism!*
[31] *Also, there's no doubt in my mind that video games and supersizing are more harmful than the beers I shared with my coaches.*

kidney stones and gallstones, hemorrhoids (oy!!!), hernias, high blood pressure, high cholesterol, heart disease, and ulcers.

The next two lists should give you some idea of what to eat. The first features foods rich in protein: beef, chicken breast, fish, turkey, cheese, cottage cheese, eggs, milk, yogurt, peanuts, sunflower seeds, beans, and lentils. The second includes many of the fiber-rich foods: bananas, apples, oranges, strawberries, peaches, apricots, prunes, and pears; carrots, peas, canned corn, broccoli, and tomato sauce; wheat bread, bran muffins, saltines, graham crackers, granola bars, raisin bran, Fig Newtons, and oatmeal; cranberry juice, apple juice, and orange juice; maple syrup, low-fat milk, and yogurt; rice and baked potatoes; and baked beans, kidney beans, black beans, and lentils.

"Fiber keeps calories moving through your system faster," Kleiner advises. "Plus, it makes you feel full."

Ah, so what she means to say is, as your metabolism slows down, you can compensate by eating more fiber. Kind of like that divide-by-five compensation rule that's a part of my annual cholesterol count formula!

Before playing football, I like to have breakfast. Generally, I'm pretty miserable if I'm hungry. And if I'm hungry and miserable, I'm not going to enjoy my time on the gridiron, am I? So I make sure to have a bowl of cereal or some eggs. However, the more important intake comes *after* I come home. I always have at least one banana, as nothing in the world sucks more than the middle-of-the-night leg cramp. Potassium helps to fight this, so I have the banana and drink some Gatorade.[32] Orange juice, prune juice (not too much!), broccoli, baked potatoes with the skin, and red snapper are other good

---

[32] *Gatorade, and other like-minded sports drinks, are composed of water, carbs, and electrolytes. We lose electrolytes when we sweat and this is a good way of replacing them. I have to hang my sweats up to dry when I get home—socks and hat too—so I know I've lost a lot of sweat and salt (sodium is an electrolyte) while playing.*

sources of potassium. We are talking breakfast, though, so the banana in a bowl of Lucky Charms and a tall glass of Gatorade is just what the doctor ordered. But if you fall prey to frequent charley horses, you might want to go a step further.

Dr. Michael Klaper, a nutritional specialist, writes, "Frequent leg cramps are often a sign of an electrolyte imbalance. I believe that part of the answer is to increase your intake of calcium and magnesium."

Dr. Klaper recommends eating green, leafy vegetables like broccoli and kale for these vitamins. Another good source is calcium-fortified orange juice. Low-fat dairy products, sardines with bones (yummy! crunchy!), nuts, beans, and whole grains are also good. But let's say it's three in the morning and all of a sudden there's a fist squeeze, squeeze, squeezing inside your calf. For those of you who don't keep a bushel of kale handy on the night table, get ready to massage. Flop out of bed without waking the wife, sit on the floor, and pull the cramped leg up to your chest, bending it at the knee. Push your thumb gently into your calf, hold it there, and breathe normally until the cramp begins to relax. If this doesn't work, put your hands on either side of the cramp and roll the muscle from left to right. If this doesn't work, take two shots of tequila and call me in the morning.

Seriously, though, if this is a recurrent problem, direct intake of vitamins might be the preventive medicine that your body needs. Vitamin E should be used to supplement daily dosages of up to 1,000 milligrams of magnesium and up to 1,000 milligrams of calcium. On a related note, the vitamin and mineral supplement business has grown now to sales of more than $3 billion per year. And guess what? If you eat healthy and live an active life, most of these supplements are unnecessary. When you eat decently, you get vitamins. That being said, adults, especially men, can use a daily dose of antioxidants. Vitamin C (citrus fruits, berries, and green leafy veggies), vitamin E (nuts and seeds), and beta-carotene (carrots, sweet pota-toes, spinach, broccoli, and fruit)—all considered antioxidants—can reduce the risk of cancer and heart disease. They also reduce the risk of tissue damage, which will keep you active and in the huddle!

Each day, I take three pills, and it makes me feel like a schmuck. But because Dr. Epstein and his nurse practitioner, Jana, are smarter than me and because I want to live long enough to run a crisp down and in (and maybe even catch the ball!) on my hundredth birthday, I listen. Despite the occasional fish-tasting burp, each morning I swallow a horse pill for my Omega-3 needs, along with a big ol' vitamin C. At night, before bed, I have my Lipitor. And in between, three or four Advil to keep the back from barking. I'm sure that I could cut a pill or two if I eased up on the melted cheese and dropped twenty pounds. That still wouldn't get me to my ideal weight, but it would certainly chase the fish taste from my mouth.

Speaking of which, it's easy enough to determine your ideal weight if you follow a formula even more simple than my drink-a-beer and divide-by-five equation. I stand six feet tall and weigh anywhere from 210 (midsummer) to 220 (post-holidays). According to the formula, I am thirty to forty pounds overweight. Although I look nothing like John Candy or Chris Farley, I am considered "obese." I don't feel obese. I don't look obese. Richard Simmons has never run up behind me in search of a hug and reaffirmation. However, these doctors and nutritionists have little to gain from painting me as a fat person, so there has to be some method to their madness. Now, the formula: men are allowed 106 pounds for their first five feet of height. For every inch above that, you may add six pounds. So, for me, my ideal weight, at six feet tall, is 178 pounds. (Gimme a break—that's what I weighed as a seventh-grade moron!!!) For women, it's one hundred pounds and an additional five pounds per inch above five feet. Just to be fair, doctors and nutritionists and guys like Mr. French

Fries give some leeway. If you're 10 percent above or below, they say you're A-OK. And if you can burn two hundred and fifty to five hundred calories a day, you can lose a pound every week. Three thousand five hundred calories equals one pound of body fat. Burn calories and shed those pounds like you shed blockers!

It's all about forming good habits. Now—we all know that everyone says to form good habits at a young age. The problem is, it's rare to find a young person who wants to listen to anything an old person has to say. I'll admit, by the time I saw the wisdom of their ways, I was amongst them! If only we could combine the wisdom of the aged and the vigor of youth . . .

Not only should you live life, you should live it enthusiastically. Doctors, nutritionists, advice columnists, and Mr. French Fries all agree. Be passionate. Be actively engaged. Be enthusiastic. Don't allow the years, let alone the ass kicking that is full-time employment, home ownership, and parenthood slow you down. Make sure to make time for yourself. And be passionate about the things you do. There's nothing wrong with an increased heart rate when the excitement is directed toward positive, productive activity. You know, like flying across the field in pursuit of a scrambling quarterback or leaping skyward to haul in a Hail Mary. When you wake up in the morning, you ought to be able to hop out of bed with your heart racing in anticipation. There should be at least one thing that puts a smile on your face, something that even if you don't do it well, you do it with chutzpah.

I wholeheartedly embrace coffee and bagels and even the occasional donut, but there are thirty other meals that can be handled with more care every week. Eat smart at home and you can go out with the fellas and enjoy all of the baked goods you want; all that talk of Hail Marys and goal line stands, too.

10

The "Not Quite Ready for Canton Players": The Men of Bartlett One

ollege meant all of the joys, all of the highs, and unfortunately, some of the lows, of intramural football. Our team—consisting of the residents of Bartlett One, plus the four or five stragglers who slept in the common room—was decent, but nothing to write home about. Nor was it worth it to write home when I sprained my knee badly enough for crutches. No need to give Mom something to worry about. I'd save that for report card time!

The knee thing was a bummer, as it happened the week before the Mini Quad Super Bowl, where eight teams played in a tournament with all of the idiocy and fun culminating in a Super Bowl on Sunday. Friday night kicked off with a couple of cases of Genesee Cream Ale (kind of like those pasta dinners in high school, but just a little different). On Saturday morning, my men, and they *were* my men now as I had taken on the role of coach—lucky fish tie, whistle, clipboard, and all—fought through their hangovers with an all-you-can-eat breakfast before taking the field for the first game.[33] As luck would have it we were matched up with the jock floor. Comprised of a bunch of lacrosse players and led by a fifth-year student (their RA) who'd played defensive end on the football team, we figured to get killed. And through the first half, it *was* murder.

As we gathered in the common room during the five-minute halftime, I dealt with the fact that my fastest man, Fred, had been asleep on the sidelines for most of the game. At Dixon's suggestion, I nursed him back to health with a beer. Next, I instructed my defensive backs to forget about the man-to-man and play a zone. Bob was tall and quick, so he would switch from corner to deep safety. I told him, "Play center field like you've never played center field before!" We took the ball at our own twenty and the ref, the Dean of Student Life (he'd have to call my roommate and me in "for a little chat" a few months later), blew the whistle. We were off and running, and as LL Cool J says, "Don't call it a comeback!"

It was their offense stalling now as Bob cut off all deep routes. They ran a couple short slants underneath, but our middle linebacker, a dread-headed dude named Dewey, knew to drop back into coverage. About this time, my roommate Mike started connecting with his passes. He'd lost a finger in a snowblower accident a few years before, but no matter. He saw the field well and the Cream Ale had finally exited his system . . . just as it was reentering Fred's! Streaking, streaking, streaking down the sidelines, three straight fly patterns resulted in three straight touchdowns. Before the third quarter had ended, we were all tied

---

[33] *No training table is complete without chocolate chip pancakes and bacon, bacon, bacon!!!*

up. They went ahead for a few minutes before we put the ball in twice more. Game over.

There was another victory in the afternoon and then a celebration of Genesee Cream Ale and chicken wings. Going to school near Buffalo may be tough during those long winter months, but there are some benefits, buffalo wings being first and foremost. As we tore through cups of bleu cheese and cases of Cream Ale, I awarded the game ball to Bobo, Darby, and Springer. They'd given Mike plenty of time to throw, and it's important to recognize those who all too often go unrecognized. (A team will never be any better than its offensive line, and you don't have to be Vince Lombardi to know that!) This was the second of our Team Unity meals and there would be two more the following day, including, yes indeed, a championship dinner.

For that, we upgraded to Piels!

Bob got Sunday's game ball, as he played stellar D. He also caught the game-winning touchdown in the morning game, as well as the afternoon rematch with the lacrosse players and their rambunctious RA.[34] That game gave us the trophy and the undying respect of the Dean of Student Life. At least until February, when he threatened to kick Mike and me out of school if we didn't cool it with the drinking games. Apparently, he was a bigger fan of football than Quarters and Anchorman.

Sunday nights were always fun—backgammon tournaments, cards, movies, guys taking their weekly shower, procrastinating on homework—and this one especially so. Before bed, everybody gave the lucky fish tie a touch, and then we nailed it to the wall in commemoration. It would soon be joined by that warning letter from the dean—a letter that, like the championship itself, became an instant source of pride for the men of Bartlett One.

[34] Not since Flutie to Phelan had two dorm mates hooked up on such an important pass!

And the inductees are . . .
The men of Bartlett One, along with an
honorable mention for Little Feat, whose
"Dixie Chicken" was the team song.
"And all the boys there, at the bar,
began to sing along . . . "

11

Workin' on Strategy and Skills While Still Payin' the Bills

It was sometime during high school, sometime during the Big '80s, that I first took note of all the TV contracts and Madison Avenue influence in professional football. It never should have gone further than that feel-good toss from Mean Joe Greene—everything since (outside of Payton high-fiving accountants, Donovan taking a breather in the Philly cold, and the Michael Vick experience) has come across as very contrived. Advertising led to all too much self-promotion, and now we've got to watch Joe Horn audition for cellular companies and Terrell Owens for Bic.

I'll admit, I'm a bit bitter over the fact that T.O. earns with one catch what I make in a year. The truth is, he can be a head case because he's got the talent to get away with it. Weekend warriors do not. That being said, we wouldn't be able to play if we didn't do a couple of things right, such as crisp patterns or pressure on the quarterback or just great one-liners at opportune times. We've obviously got a little bit of talent and skill, but there are always things to work on if we want to continue contributing, and as was mentioned earlier, time can be as much of a problem as health. In the perfect world, Saturday would be twenty-six hours long instead of a mere twenty-four. Between eight A.M. and ten A.M., all family members, including pets, would continue to sleep while we played. The alarm clock would be the garage door opening upon your return or, better yet, the shower turning off as you stepped out. Then and only then would the day begin, that is, at least family-wise.

And as a perfect world bonus, every Wednesday would be a half-day with the freedom to do whatever physical activity you wanted in the afternoon. Ah, then we'd be in good shape, wouldn't we? Sometimes, we get something closely resembling that perfect world. But the truth is that sometimes is called sometimes because it only happens some of the time. And if you're like me and can't have "all of the time," well then, you've got to get your exercise while working on your skills while playing your game (while still paying your bills).

I'll begin with the pursuit of El Gato: "El Gato is a legend, known all across the land. For El Gato is the fastest, he is the fastest man. El Gato gets down the field, before you can bat an eye. His name might say he is a cat, but El Gato he can fly." I could go on, but I won't. Simply put, we all want to be El Gato. We all want to be quick as a cat. But as long as we are relatively fast and have legs and lungs we can rely on, we'll just have to be happy with that. What would probably do us the most good is twenty minutes a day of shuttlecock. That's right, shuttlecock.[35] But we no longer have time for shuttlecock. None of us is willing or able to run suicides

---

[35] *If "shuttlecock" made you laugh, congratulations. You're as immature as I am!*

while transporting little wooden blocks from one yard line to another. However, the purpose is still relevant. Quick feet. El Gato. Shuttlecock or no shuttlecock, you've got to find some way to fight the trudging turtle effect that comes with age. In basketball, without a quick first step, you can't take your man to the hole. And if you can't take your man to the hole, he can overplay against the outside shot and you'll have nuttin'. In football, without quick feet you will get abused on defense, and you won't ever touch the ball on offense because you'll be so easy to guard. You've got to spend more time on your toes, Gato.

Go for a run. Do some cross-stepping during that run. Dance with yo' happy feet! The stairs in your house? Jog up and down 'em. At the very least, walk them after a meal. Just don't trip over the dog or squash the cat. And if you live in a home without stairs or have no desire to dance in public, or, worse still, have a bad back like me, you'll just have to save the pounding for Saturdays. Find an elliptical machine at a health club or go swimming. Low-impact cardiovascular is the key if you're looking to take a minimal toll on your body. Can you walk to work? Or at least take a walk during the day? Find a way. And how about this helpful hint: When driving home from work, drive right past McDonald's. Think "Preferred Plus." Think post patterns.

Manual dexterity, better known as hand-eye coordination, is also very important. So unless you're the quarterback, hurry up and remind yourself how to watch the ball while running. It's not that easy to do, especially when you're using up all you've got just to get open. The vision tends to bounce with the heavy breathing and heavy footsteps, so run on the balls of your feet. It's like when pursuing a fly ball in baseball; if you run on your heels, that ball will bounce so much it'll make Danette Partellow's T-shirt look like a still life! There's a time and a place for visions of bounciness, and now—with you focusing on an incoming pass—is not one of them.

Find somebody and run ten-yard down-and-out patterns a couple thousand times. OK, we'll settle for fifty of them. Run them toward a sideline so you can work on stopping short of going out of bounds. Run full speed on the balls of your feet and do all you can to keep your eye on the ball. If you have a third guy, let him guard you, so that you can work on making those crucial cuts and creating some space.

The best time for this, more likely than not, will be during warm-ups. And once you start playing, there are some things that you all, as a team, can do to increase your chances of winning. Physical mistakes just can't be helped sometimes, but mental mistakes can. They can be avoided, given good planning and strategy in the Walter Camp style. It only makes sense for us to compensate: the more we slow down, the more we have to put our heads to use.

I'll begin with the start of a play. Having a relatively athletic guy at center can often pay dividends, for if your center says "Hike," he is now the quarterback.[36] If they blitz, he can just eat the ball for a minimal loss. If they don't, he can drop back and all sorts of trickery can proceed from there. One of the keys to good play-calling is keeping the defense honest. Do this with the occasional center self-snap, which can lead to him throwing the ball or pitching it to a running back, who then has the option to run or get off a quick throw. It's also wise to put someone in the backfield with the quarterback every once in a while. In smaller pickup games, most position players will line up as receivers, but there are a couple of good plays you can run with a man in the backfield, including having someone stay back to pick up the blitz. In this case, the center would probably release and run a quick out to give the QB an outlet.

---

[36] Yes, it is legal to hike to yourself.

Another offensive hint involves managing your first down, like in real football when the coach and quarterback have to manage the clock. There is no clock in our games, but we do have the solitary first down to consider. In simplest terms, if it's first or second down and the ball carrier isn't going to make it much further down the field, he will want to run out of bounds just short of the first down. (This is a definite if the defense has already used their blitz.) The offense has a shot now at a longer, riskier play with one or two downs remaining to get the first down. Often-times you will see a QB scramble away from the blitz, get some running room, but with a defensive back closing in opt for the sideline, not to avoid injury but to keep from passing the pylon and using up the one and only first down his team's got.

As far as receivers and their patterns go, whoever is calling the plays must be willing to make adjustments throughout. The guys I play with don't clamor too much about "I'm getting open every time!" in the huddle, so I can trust them when they tell me they're beating their man. To catch the defense by surprise, I might call two plays in the huddle, saving the one based on the receiver's input for the second, no-huddle play. We run the first play, rush to the line of scrimmage, hike the ball, and then try to beat them where there is a flaw. On a different but related note, it's smart to run two receivers slanting across the field, either in the same direction, with one guy ten to fifteen yards deeper than the other, or in a crossing pattern. Although picks are illegal, it can confuse a defense, whether they're in man-to-man or zone, when two guys cross paths. The other confusing dynamic duo pattern is to line up two receivers, side by side, and have them run in a straight line right at a certain spot. Let's say that spot is ten yards downfield. The first receiver might buttonhook, setting something of a screen for the second receiver, who quickly breaks in or out depending on where his man is standing. The QB knows

As a defender, the angle you take on the ball carrier is very important. In this case, Nutsy's close, so very close . . .

. . . but clearly, he has taken a bad angle. There is a speed mismatch here that the QB must've recognized when drawing up the play. Either that or Joe clued him in.

to wait for the receiver's cut before throwing the ball. This kind of distraction/picking/screening often works, as defensive play-calling rarely gets the attention that offensive play-calling does (kind of like in my freshman year with "Coach" Gilmore!).

And so, when on defense, try and mix it up a bit. If you always play man-to-man, eventually the offense will figure out where the mismatch is; they will find the seam and exploit it. If you don't mix it up with your defensive scheme, including when you blitz and who does the blitzing, the offense will take advantage. One thing I like to do once every seven or eight plays is have my rusher drop back into shallow coverage, even as he's counting his three Mississippis. This is especially useful if there's a quick scrambler of a QB and/or if the center is a good blocker. Like dread-headed Dewey in college, having this guy drop four or five yards back, while still hawking the quarterback, can often interrupt short routes like buttonhooks and slants. Speaking of slants, watch out for these when there is a man in motion. A body in motion tends to stay in motion, and a body weighed down by the years and beers will have a hard time catching up!

Earlier, I mentioned running out of bounds short of the first down. The defensive equivalent of this would be having the wherewithal to knock a desperation pass to the ground on fourth down. To intercept it so deep in your own territory is the equivalent of letting them get off a punt. Your team now has its back against the wall, stuck near the goal line, when you could be lining up at the original line of scrimmage. See? If you just use your head a little bit, you'll make up for some of those physical shortcomings!

On the theme of the following photos, when you're rushing the quarterback, remember to keep your body under control. You can't just launch into an all-out sprint because it becomes too easy for the QB to avoid you and free himself for that all-important extra two or three seconds—just long enough to wing the ball

"Bliiiitz!!!" Nutsy's got Eric all tied up, but it looks like Dr. John's going to have a straight shot at Joe (not pictured). You can rush/blitz as many as you'd like, but remember that the more you "bring," the less you'll have in the defensive backfield . . .

When rushing, try and keep those hands up. You may not get the sack, but you could prevent the QB from getting a good look downfield. In this case, Nutsy finally cut a good angle and it looks like Joe, rather than risking the INT, is just going to eat the ball.

downfield. Work on containment, which includes running with your hands up high but also out wide.

As a defensive back, you want to be all over your man. You *need* to be all over your man. The key is to know when to stop backpedaling and to turn and start running with him. The only thing you can really do is focus on his midsection, so that you don't fall for his moves. One trick that will help the winded and weary is to bump your guy at the line. Try and slow him down before he gets up a full head of steam. Just know that if you're beat tired, as soon as he gets by you, you'll be beat literally! So let your safety know that you'll be bumping at the line and may need help. Defense is all about humility. Humility and speed. Right, El Gato?

12

The "Not Quite Ready for Canton Players": Super Craiger's Perfect Spiral

Everybody's got their Turkey Bowl stories. If the field isn't the concrete and curb in front of Grandma's house, then it must be the fabled frozen tundra or, better yet, a muddy mess like Haynes Field. The players are either hungover and running at half speed, or they treat the game as their own personal Super Bowl with a whole year's worth of bragging rights on the line. Either way, football on Thanksgiving morning is a great American tradition. I mean, what better way to enjoy your turkey than with a torn tendon? Sore quads and hammies? A groin that twangs like country music every time you shift in your seat? A lump the size of Aunt Hilda's deviled eggs atop your head? Fingers so mangled you can't even pull on the wishbone?

A few years after college, eight of us gathered to play—all friends from high school, in old sweats and not a pair of cleats in sight. There'd been a Barn Party the night before, so the game started out slow, but things picked up a bit when Craig got picked off. Sending JP on the first deep route of the day, he heaved a bomb, only to watch it fall into Don's hands. (Oh beautiful irony, as Don is JP's brother; score another one for the younger brothers!) Don ran it all the way back for a touchdown as I blocked Craig, the only possible tackler on my teammate's road to glory. As we untangled our arms and legs, I deadpanned, "Sweet pass, man." Amazingly, Craig skipped right over the sarcasm, not to mention the INT, and said, "I know. I'm feelin' good!"

Apparently, Super Craiger was so happy to be tossing the pigskin again that he'd completely glossed over the fact that his pass had come down five yards short, was intercepted, and then returned for a touchdown. As he got the ball back for another set of downs, he even had the nerve to add, "Did you see that spiral? Beautiful . . . "

I had no choice, sports fans. Skipping the obligatory three Mississippis, I blitzed, tackled him to the ground, and momentum saw us both roll right over his throwing hand. Unfortunately, Craig would not be scooping mashed potatoes up with his right hand that afternoon. I'd broken his pinky. When he finally got up off of the ground, the thing was bent like a goalpost after the crowd has tired of trying to rip it down. I believe all he could say then was, "Ow."

I did feel badly about the break, worse still about the fact that we had uneven teams now and needed to play with an ineligible center. Fortunately, injuries are a rarity in the pickup pigskin games that I play. I think it's because we do a respectable job of mixing common sense with competition. There was Super Craiger's pinky and Dr. John shredded a groin last winter, and Joe sprains his ankle every week, but other than that—knock on wood!—there have been very few trips to the doctor's office for me and my boys. Just the occasional need to "pass" on the wishbone—right, Craig?

> **And the inductees are . . .**
> JP and family for hosting all those Barn Parties and for being so dedicated to Big Blue that they watch tapes of regular-season Giants games from years past. Frequently.[37]

---

[37] *Even the Mara family doesn't do that!!!*

13

Know When to Say When: Throwing the Flag and Talkin' a Good Game

When angry at the ref(s) for screwing my Giants, I've been known to yell at the television. The only thing that calms me is the realization—begrudging, like the kid who waits three hours to admit he broke the vase—that our linemen can't block theirs without using a lasso, electrical tape, and a bear trap, and that, OK, the referee wasn't completely wrong. Then I get mad at our offensive line for causing another twenty-yard completion to be called back and start yelling at the TV again. A vicious cycle, indeed.

Nowadays, the games we're playing don't include a zebra. We've got to regulate ourselves and call our own penalties. I really think this is an art form; it's a subtlety requiring you to read setting, characters, and plot. Wait, no . . . That would be reading as in reading a book. But actually, now that I think about it, that's exactly what you have to do when deciding whether to call a penalty. You need to figure out what kind of game you're in and this, of course, depends on where you're playing (setting), the other players (characters), and what has happened up to that point (plot). Some places, the rule is "no blood, no foul." In other places, the guys will call penalties on themselves, kind of like in the "old school" approach in basketball when the guilty party raises his hand to give his coach and the scorer notice. I'm sure there are also some prima donnas out there who will call every little thing. "Flag! He got mud on my new jersey!" This whining is ten times worse than when you complain about an injury, obviously. Luckily, none of the fellas I play with fall into this category. They all welcome mud on the jersey.

Generally, we only call blatant penalties. If further definition is needed, when I say blatant I mean that 1) I stood a very good chance of catching the ball before you inflicted bodily harm on me, or 2) your intent *was* to inflict bodily harm! My own personal rule is that if I could still catch the ball but dropped it, I won't call the pass interference. I've yet to really tick anyone off or have my integrity called into question, so you might want to let this rule be your guide.

Paul did try and slow me down once, questioning my Mississippi count, but it was just gamesmanship. Ah, gamesmanship . . . A pretty fitting term to describe the banter of big men in big moments. It's one part psychology, one part word play, three parts heart, and five parts savvy. To better prepare you for combat, the following is a list of the words and phrases most often used on the gridiron. Never again will you be unable to respond to a haze because you have no idea what it means. Never again will you have to succumb to somebody's gamesmanship while searching for a dictionary! You are about to experience a vocabulary upgrade, my friend.

GOIN' BACK TO SCHOOL: A LESSON IN FOOTBALL VOCABULARY

1. Audible: Verbal commands shouted by the quarterback to his teammates at the line of scrimmage so as to change a play on short notice.
2. Backfield: The area behind the line of scrimmage where the running backs roam.
3. Backs: The running backs (i.e., the halfback and fullback).
4. Beat: When a player lets the guy he's guarding get past him. If you're looking to haze a buddy, try: "You got beat like a drum!"
5. Blitz: When the defensive team sends a player rushing past the line of scrimmage and towards the QB as soon as the ball is snapped (rather than counting three Mississippis).
6. Blocking: The act of preventing a defensive player from getting to the ball carrier; blockers use their arms and bodies, but may not hold the defensive player with their hands.
7. Bomb: A long pass thrown to a receiver sprinting down the field.
8. Bowl game: A postseason football game played between two successful teams. Or, in the case of college football, two teams that have records hovering around .500 but very, very influential alumni. Anyone else hungry for Tostidos? For Poulan Weed Eater?[38]

---

[38] *References to just two of the ridiculously named bowl games. When oh when will college football follow a format similar to March Madness?!?!*

Football Facts

College bowl games have a long tradition, and here is one that I can relate to: According to sports historian Vic Frolund, when the Michigan Wolverines crushed the Stanford Cardinal 49–0 in the inaugural Rose Bowl on January 1, 1902, Michigan used the same eleven players the entire game, never once substituting. The three players who didn't get into the game were so embarrassed that before going home, they put their uniforms back on and rolled in the mud!

9. Bump-and-run: When pass defenders hit a receiver within five yards of the line of scrimmage to slow him down.

10. Burned: When a defensive back gets "beat." If you're looking to haze a buddy, try: "You got burned like toast on that play!"

11. Clipping: Blocking an opponent below the waist from behind; this illegal block is a personal foul, punishable by a fifteen-yard penalty and death by dismemberment.

12. Complete pass: A forward pass to a teammate who catches it in the air.

13. Cover(age): Preventing a player from gaining yards; in pass coverage, a defender follows a receiver to prevent him from catching a pass.

14. Cut back: A sudden change in direction taken by an offensive

player to make it more difficult for defenders to guard him.

15. Dead ball: A ball becomes dead when a play is over (the ball ends up on the ground or the offensive player is "tackled"), and becomes live as soon as it is snapped for the next play.

16. Double coverage: When two defensive players cover one receiver.

17. Down: One of four chances the offensive team has to gain a first down. Also, when the ball carrier is tackled, or, in our case, two-hand touched.

18. Downfield: In the direction of the goal line; the offense is always trying to get downfield.

19. Drive: The series of plays a team puts together in an attempt to score.

20. Drop back: When after the snap the quarterback takes a few steps backward into an area called the pocket so as to pass the ball.

21. Eligible receiver: A player allowed by the rules to catch a forward pass; all offensive players are eligible, except linemen, and sometimes even they can be eligible.

The numbers were low on this snowy day, so it was a two-on-three with an ineligible center. At least, until I finished taking my photos!

22. End zone: The area between the end line and goal line bounded by the sidelines, which a team on offense tries to enter so as to score a touchdown.[39]

23. Field position: The location of a team on the field relative to the two goal lines; good field position means to be near the opponent's goal line, while bad field position is to be backed up against your own.

24. First down: The first out of four chances that the offensive team has to put the ball into the end zone or merely move it past the marker that will grant them a second set of four downs. We only allow one first down, marked by a pylon halfway down the field.

25. Forward pass: A pass thrown downfield; a team is allowed to throw only one forward pass per play, and it must be thrown from behind the team's line of scrimmage.

26. Forward progress: The location to which a ball carrier has advanced the ball, even if he was pushed backwards after getting there.

27. Foul: A violation of football's rules by a team or player, punishable by a penalty (something like docking pay or administering a wedgie).

28. Fumble: When a ball carrier loses possession by dropping the ball or having it knocked away before a play ends.

29. Goal line: A line drawn across the width of the field, which a team must cross with the ball to score a touchdown. And for defensive excitement, there really is nothing quite like the goal line stand!!!

30. Going for it: When a team facing a fourth down decides to try for the first down instead of punting; if it fails, the team

[39] Unless you are a recent immigrant trying to convert from fútbol to football, I say shame on you for not knowing this!

loses possession of the ball. "You going for it?" is one of the most frequently asked questions during a game. Even more popular than the ubiquitous, "One more trip up and back."

31. Hand-off: A running play where the quarterback hands the ball to a running back.

32. Holding: A foul where a player impedes the movement of an opponent by grasping or hooking any part of his body; punishable by a penalty—specific yardage in organized games, a loss of down in our game.

33. In-bounds: The region of the field inside the sidelines and end lines.

34. Incomplete pass: A forward pass that touches the ground before being caught. As Tom Cruise says, "You incomplete me . . . "

35. Intentional grounding: A foul called against a quarterback who purposely throws an incomplete pass so as to avoid a sack.

36. Interception: A pass caught in the air (picked off) by a defender whose team immediately gains possession of the ball and becomes the offense.

37. Lateral: A backward pass thrown to a teammate; unlike a forward pass (which can be thrown only once per play), players may lateral the ball as often as they want. Remember that Stanford play with the marching band!

38. Line of scrimmage: An imaginary line that no player may cross before the snap; each team has its own line of scrimmage, separated by the neutral zone (one yard wide).

39. Lineman: A player who starts each play at the line of scrimmage, either rushing the passer or protecting him.

40. Live ball: A ball becomes live as soon as it is snapped.

41. Loose ball: A ball that is not in possession of either team, such as after a fumble; in some games it can be recovered, while in others it is simply a dead ball.

42. Man-in-motion: A single player on the offense who is permitted

Is there anything better than lining up at the line of scrimmage in three inches of snow? Note that due to the slippery conditions, Mike is giving even more than a yard for the neutral zone.

to move prior to the snap; he may only run parallel to the line of scrimmage or away from it.

43. Midfield: The fifty-yard line, which divides the length of the field in half; forty-yard line if you're only playing eighty, like us. Midfield is where the first-down pylon can be found.

44. Offside: When any part of a player's body is beyond the line of scrimmage as the ball is snapped; a foul punishable by a five-yard penalty in organized games, but with a snowball to the head in ours.

45. On downs: The term used to describe a team's loss of possession if it fails to reach the necessary line on a fourth-down play. "Turned over on downs" is the expression used to describe this situation.

46. Open receiver: A player who has no defender closely covering him. "He was wide friggin' open!" is what a defender will hear from teammates after getting burned.

47. Out of bounds: The region of the field outside of the sidelines and end lines; as soon as a ball carrier or the ball itself goes out of bounds, the play is over.

48. Pass defender: A defensive player who covers an opposing receiver.

49. Pass patterns: The routes that receivers follow to help the quarterback quickly hit them with a pass. Sometimes guys won't run out their patterns and an astute QB will reward them by never looking their way again—at least not that day.

50. Pass protection: Blocking by offensive players to keep defenders away from the quarterback on passing plays.

51. Pass rush: A horde of defenders—even if it's just one guy named Nutsy—whose sole goal is to kill the quarterback.

52. Personal foul: A foul that might cause injury; punishable by a fifteen-yard penalty in organized games and by personal embarrassment in the "Letters to the Editor" section of our town paper when it happens to us.[40]

53. Picked off: Intercepted. Like Craig.

54. Pitch-out: A lateral tossed from a quarterback to a running back.

55. Play-action pass: A passing play after the quarterback has faked a hand-off. This is done to draw in the defense before trying to go long.

56. Pocket: The area behind the offensive line where the quarterback feels safe and secure because he is protected by his blockers.

57. Possession: Sometimes used to say which player has the ball and sometimes used to say which team is currently on offense.

58. Previous spot: Where the ball was snapped to begin the last play. Important for all those judicious do-overs!

59. Pylon: A short orange marker at each of the end zone's four corners (for a total of eight pylons; and don't forget the two for the first down).

---

[40] On par with having your child named in the police blotter!

Al drops a pylon in place, but doesn't drop a pass. Ever![41]

In warm-ups, even those who always play on the line can dream of quarterback glory. Nutsy obviously has such dreams!

[41] *I made this the caption rather than pointing out how important pylons are on snowy days because I didn't want to insult your intelligence.*

60. Quarterback: Overpaid, overconfident guy who can throw the ball like Robin Hood shoots arrows. The leader of a team's offense, he takes the snap from the center and either hands the ball to a running back, runs with it himself, or passes it to a receiver. Most will get the ball off faster than Nutsy (see previous photo!)

61. Reading the defense: Recognition by the quarterback of the defensive formation; he may then call an audible to adjust the offense.

62. Receiver: An offensive player whose job is to get open, catch the ball, then run like the wind into the end zone!

63. Recovery: To gain or regain possession of a fumble.

64. Red zone: The imaginary area between the defense's twenty-yard line and its goal line from which the offense is most likely to score points.

65. Return: An attempt by a player who has just caught an interception, punt, or kickoff to advance the ball the other way. In weekend warrior football, though, it is most often heard in question form—"Do you think he'll ever return?"—after a guy limps to his car and leaves.

66. Roll out: When a quarterback runs parallel to the line, buying himself more time and looking for an open receiver.

67. Rush: Another name for a running play, on offense, or for putting pressure on the quarterback when on defense.

68. Sack: A tackle of the quarterback behind his line of scrimmage. "Tackle" meaning two-hand touch, fellas. Go easy on the pretty boy!

69. Safety: When a ball carrier is tackled in his own end zone after bringing the ball there under his own power; the defense earns two points in regular regulation football, but only a half-point for us.

70. Scrambling: The hectic movements by a quarterback to avoid being sacked.

71. Series: The group of four downs a team has to advance the ball past the first-down markers, or, if there are no first-down options left, into the end zone.

72. Sideline: The boundary line that runs the length of the field along each side; a ball carrier or ball that touches or crosses the sideline is out of bounds.

73. Snap: When the center, while facing forward, quickly passes the ball between his legs to the quarterback to start each play. "Hike!"

74. Spike: When a player throws the ball at the ground to celebrate a touchdown. Not cool. "Act like you've been there," is generally the company line, and well it should be. So sayeth Barry Saunders.

75. Spiral: The spin that allows a football to fly far and straight; the tighter the spiral, the farther it will go.[42]

76. Spot: A location on the field where forward progress was stopped or a foul was committed.

77. Stiff arm (or straight arm): A push by a ball carrier to ward off a tackler. Think of the Heisman Trophy.

78. Touchdown: The happy place.

79. Turnover: The involuntary loss of possession of the ball during a play, either by a fumble or by throwing an interception.

80. Zone defense: Rather than covering receivers, man-to-man, the defensive backs are responsible for an area.

So there you have it: eighty definitions for eighty yards. One for each yard you will defend on defense or, if you prefer, one for each yard you will gain on offense. Play a lot and talk even more. It's one of the joys of the game.

---

[42] *When I start tossing up knuckleballs, this is when we go to the bullpen and Tom takes over. The unwritten rule is that whoever has the tightest spiral gets to QB.*

NOTE:

You may have noticed a winter wonderland theme to the photos. That's because on a cold and snowy day, gamesmanship and banter are of the utmost importance. All of that talk helps keep us warm!

14

The "Not Quite Ready for Canton Players": Preseason Pigskin

You have to really love football to sit and watch a preseason NFL game. And you have to really, really love football to go see it live and in person.

The fellas I fell in with here in town don't just like to play sports. They have an insatiable athletic appetite that, naturally, includes attending games. Tucker, Cabbage, and I had the misfortune of bearing witness to the end of "The Curse" as the Yankees let the Red Sox burglarize the House That Ruth Built.[43] And as further proof of our willingness to witness the ridiculous, a bunch of my fellow weekend warriors and I decided to scalp preseason Giants tickets last year. We

---

[43] *The wife was there, too. She, much to my delight, is a diehard fan of the Bronx Bombers. On the other hand, she's a Pats fan. Ugh.*

are a desperate, pitiful lot, but you cannot argue this one point: We know a good time when it comes our way.

Opportunity knocked in the form of an e-mail and I said yes. I always say yes. I can't even spell __, let alone take the time to bother to type it! Simply put, I am a slut for fun. So it was on a Thursday night that six of us piled into an SUV and headed south through rush-hour traffic to The Meadowlands. The drive took two and a half hours and we missed most of the first half, but there wasn't any complaining. Not even from the morons in the back.

I should know because yes, as you would expect, I was one of those morons. This, the punishment for being picked up last! So, Mike and I had the physical misfortune of sitting in the scrunched-up third row; it was hell on the back but bountiful on the belly because right behind us was . . . the cooler! Ah, those Maroon memories.

Jonathan drove and upon arrival, we met up with his brother, Andrew, who was a definite MVP. No mere Coach's Award for a guy who, despite taking a bus over from New York City, is willing to carry buckets of Kentucky Fried Chicken. Not to mention stogies. "Chow down then stoke up, boys. We *are* husbands on parole!"

The bad news for Jonathan and Andrew was that Mike and I had pretty much finished all of the beer. There was some revenge as, toward the end of the drive Jonathan refused to pull into the Vince Lombardi rest area for a bathroom break. Still, Mike and I, feeling a benevolent combination of giddy and guilty, bought them a couple of beers as soon as we got inside Giants Stadium. By the time we sat down, it was one minute till the half and our team was being whupped by the Ravens—a sign of things to come in an awful season. We knew we'd missed the good stuff as after the first quarter the regulars headed for the showers and the sixth-stringers took over, but we were lucky enough to still get a couple of highlights (neither of which involved the Giants).

First, the Pop Warner game played on the field at halftime was phenomenal. There was a completed pass—no easy feat for eight-year-olds playing in front of 60,000 people—and even a tackle-breaking gallop into the end zone. Sufficiently limber with beer, KFC, and those cigars, we rose as one and cheered our hearts out. We were not alone either. It being Weekend Eve and all, the entire crowd got behind the kids.

The other football highlight came after the game was over. None of us was ready to squeeze back into Jonathan's truck, so we played a little pickup. If you've ever taken a look at a parking lot after a game or concert, it is a wasteland of burnt-out charcoal (one end zone), bags of trash (the other end zone), and broken beer bottles (first down!). Who needs pylons? The refuse of the masses was perfect for our pigskin needs.

With the game tied and Jonathan's keys jingling in his pocket, Joe showed his dedication by running full tilt toward a parked car, in pursuit of a pass. The door was open, so he had no choice but to slide under it to avoid decapitation. While inspecting Joe's torn jeans, Tom noticed that his waistband was elastic. Elastic waistband jeans and it wasn't even Thanksgiving! Human ingenuity strikes again.

We cut Joe some slack, though, given all of the blood—not to mention the fact that he'd held onto the ball—and decided we'd better get going before someone really got hurt. We'd be playing again on Saturday, after all.

And the inductees are . . .
Jonathan (for driving), Andrew
(for supplying), and Joe (for diving).

15

You've Got Game, But No Idea Where to Play It

I will admit that I probably wouldn't get out to play as often if not for the persistence of Paul and his e-mails. We play on a great turf field at the high school and actually have some pretty good games: two-hand touch for approximately two hours and coffee at The Beanery when we're done. And the pregame, well, it's a nice time for stretching out and catching up. We each go through our little routine, set up the pylons, then toss the pigskin till everyone's ready. This is football I can live with!

I run, I jump, I catch, I fall down, I get up, I run, and I fall down again. Some days I'm cold, some days I get wet, some days I'm just plain sweaty. In between plays I get to blow snot out of my nose; much easier now that I don't have to aim it through a face mask! When we screw up, we bust each other's chops. When we score, we try to hide our smiles.

Now, it may be that you can only get together with your boys for this kind of fun once a month. This is the only time that a lot of guys can afford to get free. For many, once a month is all that their bodies can take, "Preferred Plus" or otherwise. Well, if it's going to be just once every four or five weeks, so be it. Earmark this outing as "personal time." Like when the wife says, "I know a manicure might seem silly, but it's important to me. It's personal time." Well, she's right. She's right to go and she's right to categorize it as such. And so, my friend, are you! Just be sure to put that date on the family calendar as soon as you know when it is. Be sure to have someone leave a reminder on your answering machine, the week before; something to make everybody from the wife to the kids to the family pooch aware of your plans. And be sure to do the same for others.

There are also some who see the once-a-monthers as lucky bastards. This is because they're the poor saps who only get out to play (brace yourselves, people . . .) once a year. My sympathies.

With you annual warriors, we move past "personal time" and into the easily defensible zone most commonly referred to as "tradition." And as everyone knows, traditions cannot be messed with. It's a shame when people get divorced, but no judge—man or woman—will find you at fault if your separation came about because a tradition had to be defended. I mean, without tradition we wouldn't have any traditions. Nothing would be traditional. Words like annual and yearly would fade from our lexicon, and soon thereafter so would calendars. What reason would there be to care about anything fun that happens on a relatively regular basis, if not for tradition?

Need one? Then start a tradition of your own. And rest easy knowing that when you get that "second annual" game under

your belt, you're home free, because once you've established a tradition, nobody can take it away from you.[44]

On the flip side, there are those of you fortunate enough to
live in areas that have organized leagues. So, none of this gather-
ing of the decrepit and debilitated will be necessary—just flags!
The best source I found for information is this site: *http://www.flag-
football.org/Flag%20Football%20Links.htm*. If a league exists
within earshot of your house, the folks at flagfootball.org know
about it! Just like in those college intramurals you will find good
games, conducted in a more official manner. The most popular
variety of organized weekend warrior football seems to be eight-
on-eight flag. Sounds good to me!

Whether your game is organized for you as part of a league or
done in the pickup style on a weekly, monthly, or annual basis,
always look for new blood for your team. Many a diehard has
even gone so far as to hook a teamless player up with their needy
opponent, just to keep things going! It's a necessary evil as, over
time, guys move and get maimed. So always be on the lookout for
new players. This may even be how you get *in* to a game: when
you're bored at a cocktail party and stuck talking to the husband
of a friend of your wife, ask him if he knows of anything. Unless
he's the fat Parcheesi guy, his answer will come with a knowing
smile. You are amongst friends.

---

[44] *If anyone from Congress is reading, feel free to add these words to the Constitution: "Once a
tradition hath been established, no one—man, woman, or child—may take it away." (Perhaps
an addendum regarding the twenty-six-hour Saturday, too.)*

16

The "Not Quite Ready for Canton Players": The E-mail Motivator

For guys like us who don't have a local flag football league, we need an organizer. We need a leader. Paul Maxwell is our E-mail Motivator.

Every posse has to have a sheriff and every circus has to have a ringleader. In high school, this was the guy who knew where the parties were. In college, he could tell you who had all of the old files. And after graduation, he was able to gather everyone at this or that bar for a reunion. Now that we've got kids and mortgages, these motivating types still manage to find ways to get folks together. Strolling in with his yellow coffee mug, pinnies, and pylons in tow, Paul has managed to keep things going for four years now.

Strike a pose . . .

Every Thursday night, his siren song looks more or less like this:

Frozen Tundra . . .

game on . . . 8:15 . . . high school . . . saturday . . . football

in or IN?

e-mail back so we know—thx—p

Ah, the choice that is not a choice; the question that is not a question: "in or IN?" The predecessor to "One more trip up and back?"

Paul utilizes both his passion for the game and his sales skills to subtly refuse all manner of no's, maybe's, and I doubt it's. You're either in or you're IN. When threatened by snow, he offers to pick up those guys who don't own a four-wheel drive.[45] When spring starts to reheat the earth, crying out for husbands of all ages to do lawn work, Paul digs deep in his bag of tricks to find more players. This year, he unearthed a bunch of med students from Yale-New Haven Hospital. Not only are there four of them, they're fast and they don't tire out in an hour's time. What a find!

And if further proof of Paul's passion is needed, he's not only available to organize and play, he'll lead the charge to The Beanery for postgame coffee, no matter how soaking wet we all are. Of course, he'll also heckle the losers into paying for everything, but that's to be expected. Who wants to be spoken to nicely after a loss? Who deserves to be?! In Paul's book as in my book as in your book, I'm sure the answer is nobody. This is what football and banter and male-bonding are all about. This is what it means to be a weekend warrior.

And the inductees are . . .
Paul the E-mail Motivator, for all of his pinnies, pylons, and peer pressure politicking. And his plaque shall read: one more trip up and back. No question mark.

---

[45] *No matter that he doesn't own one, either!*

. . . then fire away. This would be Paul's Sports Illustrated *poster, methinks!*

17

Pickup Pigskin versus Pro Ball

Sure, it'd be great if every Sunday you could play on the nation's finest fields, earning millions of dollars and the admiration of children and cheerleaders alike. But being a weekend warrior ain't so bad either. There are more than a few benefits to suburban living that life in the NFL just can't match. For example, our bodies are a little sore after a game, but from what I've read, pros bleed when they pee. Do I need to bruise my kidneys like that? I think not. And NFL linemen—well, their skin is so tight after the constant banging that you can draw blood with the touch of a Q-tip. So there's no doubt in my mind that life as a weekend warrior is better than life in the NFL. Check it out.

WHY PLAYING PICKUP PIGSKIN IS BETTER THAN PRO FOOTBALL

10. Everybody gets to be a two-way player.

9. No halftime show!

8. A cooler at midfield, while playing, on Saturday; a tailgate, before watching the pros destroy one another, on Sunday.

7. No need for a mouthguard, pads, or a cup. Chin straps, neither. I used to hate those chin-strap zits . . .

6. The field can be expanded or shrunk depending on the number of players you've got (and the severity of their collective injuries and/or hangover).

5. No double sessions or road trips and the joy of showering in your own bathroom. Alone!

4. If you need to lie down on the sidelines and take a little nap, there won't be a fine. Just the typical hazing and maybe some cold water to the head.

3. No waiting for the commercials to end whenever there's a change in possession. You may resume play just as soon as someone retrieves the ball.

2. No drug policy. ("I'm not chubby, honey. It's the 'roids!")

1. Postgame means the coffee shop rather than the media, trainer's table, and whirlpool.[46]

And did I mention tailgating?

---

[46] *Although a whirlpool sure would be nice . . .*

Nutsy and Joe work on the shotgun. When a guy switches in to center for the first time, it's common courtesy to give him a couple of practice snaps. You won't find accommodations like these in the pros!

18

Tailgating and a Return to Couchdom

ay it with me now: "Cook 'em, baby!"

There you have it, a motto for men everywhere. Whether it's a high school game on Friday, a college game on Saturday, or the real deal on Sunday, there is now a phrase to sum up all of the excitement of Game Day; all of the joys of football fun and, in particular, tailgating. "Cook 'em, baby!"

My buddy Chris is an actor, and perhaps his finest moment came last fall in a Pepsi commercial. Shot in the Giants Stadium parking lot, the theme is tailgating and Chris has the big line. While working the barbecue like Jersey's version of Emeril, he cries out in a fit of football bliss: "Cook 'em, baby!"

I once went to New Haven for the traditional rivalry that is Yale-UConn. This was as big as it got in the Nutmeg State—back in the good old days when UConn was as bad as Yale—so we all pulled into one of the fields outside of the Yale Bowl and set up shop. You'll be shocked to learn that, unlike that preseason Giants game, we never even made it inside. Nope, we stayed outside and tailgated the afternoon away. Cook 'em, we did. It was a real good time and the post-chowdown pickup game was on par with that night at the Meadowlands, minus the discovery of an elastic waistband.

When tailgating, I have a few recommendations. In case you've been out of the country since you were ten, have just recently discovered that people eat in parking lots, or are suffering through amnesia, this is how you run a pregame party.

First, get yourself a bag of charcoal. Then, be sure to have a barbecue in which to put this charcoal. (Feel free to reverse the order of these first two directives. . . .) Lighter fluid helps, too, especially if it's a big parking lot. Trailer parks attract tornadoes and stadium lots attract wind. Without lighter fluid—and a good lighter, preferably a Zippo—you will have a hard time getting that charcoal lit. Once it is, cover up and let the charcoal burn down to an ashy gray. Then . . . "Cook 'em, baby!"

I am not picky with my barbecue sauces, but here are five that have treated me right. First, though, a brief history lesson. As you could probably guess, barbecuing is a cowboy thing. No, not Jerry Jones's Cowboys, but rather the cowboys that drove cattle across the great plains and then gathered 'round the fire for some Texas Hold'em. They didn't have the best cuts of meat to bring on the trail, so they had to spice up—not to mention preserve—their brisket with some sauce. Human ingenuity strikes again. Next thing you know, guys are dipping their hot dogs into barbecue sauce and washing it down with beer. An appropriate homage paid to the original caballeros!

Fast forward now to the twenty-first century when it is near impossible to rank barbecue sauces because of the variety of tastes and the massive number available. But, I did want to name a few. My main source was the Scovie Awards, bestowed every year by *Fiery-Foods and Barbecue Magazine.*

RIGHTEOUS SAUCES

5. Dragonfart's Wet 'n' Reddy chipotle and mango barbecue sauce.[47]

4. Fighting Cock Kentucky Bourbon BBQ Sauce or Hog's Ass BBQ Sauce, both from Pepper's of Key West. (See Dragonfart footnote.)

3. Gotta have one that's a home brew, right? Try a concoction consisting of the following: ketchup, honey mustard, A.1., garlic salt, and cumin. Just do the best you can to stick with barbecue sauces that aren't high in sugar as they tend to get all gunky, maybe even burn, and definitely stick to your grill.[48]

2. Greg's Happy Sauce from the Carolina Sauce Company. This one won two Scovies!

1. Bull's-Eye Original from Garland, Texas, which is a real hotbed for barbecue sauces. And unlike some of the others I've suggested, this one can be found on the shelves of most grocery stores. It has molasses and fructose corn syrup, so flip frequently to avoid the crusty gunkies.

---

[47] *OK, I admit it. This one made it for the name. Is there any line of products out there with names more fun than BBQ and hot sauces? I think not.*

[48] *Avoiding sugar can be tough, though, as many of the world's greatest BBQ sauces are fruit-based. Be wary of the fructose and the glucose and any of the other -toses!*

If sauce is your thing, I suggest going to *www.bbqsauceofthe-month.com* for a new taste every thirty days. Whatever you come up with, the night before the big game, pour a bottle of sauce into a Ziploc, add the meat, chicken, or whatever, and let the marinating begin. And if you forget to do this or if it's game day and you don't want to have to mind the grill too closely, simply pour the sauce on after the food's done cooking as you would with any other condiment. Yummy.

Football Facts

If you want to go the rub route, Stubb's (out of Austin, Texas) is the one I recommend. I'd also swear by McCormick's Montreal Steak Seasoning in a court of law.

Next tip: Get bags of ice for your coolers. Oh yes, you must have coolers.

Perhaps the plural is not necessary, but I think it is. Even if you only have four people, you will want a cooler for all of the food and another for all of the beer. Mmmmm, beer. Although I dig a nice heavy beer like an Anchor Steam or a Sierra Nevada and even the occasional Half and Half (Guinness and Bass), when it comes to tailgating, I need something lighter. No need for my beer to sit like a meal at a quarter to noon on a Sunday morning! But first, the accoutrements, the accessories, the side dishes, the hors . . .

ANALOGY: CHIPS ARE TO TAILGATES AS LINEMEN ARE TO OFFENSES

5. Doritos of any variety.

4. Sun Chips, preferably Harvest Cheddar.

3. Cheese Puffs. The ones that are more compact are good, too. You know, the Cheese Doodles.

2. Ruffles in the pillow-sized bag.

1. Pringles. Not only are they the saltiest, everybody can walk around with their own tube. It's like drinking your beer— simply tilt skyward and have at it, man! No other container provides crumb management like Pringles.

You might also want to go the chips and salsa route. If you do, why not spice it up a bit with a nice black bean dip or some such? While researching the barbecue sauces, I stumbled across two dips that I will be trying out in the very near future: Jalapeño

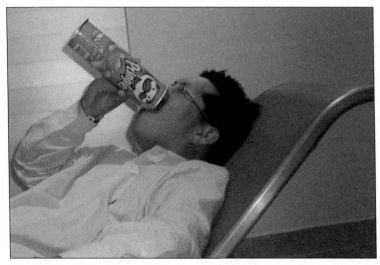

Marv tailgated so hard, he couldn't even stand up during his late night Pringles fix!!!

Black Bean Dip and Habanero Baked Bean Mix, both from the Old Fart Baked Bean Company. Hot flava, but cool dips. And how about some fruit (or are they considered a vegetable?!) to stay healthy? Pepperoncinis are a great source of vitamin C and can be hotter than a Texas summer on the tongue. Peppers good enough to qualify for my tailgate! And now it's time to wash it all down with a few beers.

CLOTHES MAY MAKE THE MAN, BUT BEER MAKES THE TAILGATE

5. Coors[49]
4. Red Stripe, Heineken, or Corona with lime (depending on which part of the world you feel like celebrating)
3. Bud Light
2. PBR, Genesee Cream Ale, Old Milwaukee, or Piels (if cheap beverages are your thing!)
1. Coors Light

Speaking of beer, I have a bonding activity for you and your teammates. The way you play is the "team" stands in a circle and passes a beer around, not to be put down until it's finished. But you don't just hand it to the next guy, you hike it between your legs, shouting out "Hike!" whenever the exchange is about to be made. If there are six of you playing, then six beers might be shared this way. Why should rugby be the only prolate spheroid sport to have drinking traditions?!?!

Now, I know that we can't all make it to every game. Trust me, I know. (I'm the guy who was happy to see the second half of a preseason game, remember?) So, for those times that you can't

---

[49] *If it's good enough for The Bandit (screw Smokey!), it's good enough for me.*

get out to the tailgate, bring the party into your own home.

Whether it's the regular season or the postseason, pro or college, nothing enhances the football-watching experience like good eats. You've seen what I think of the various chips, beers, and barbecue sauces. Now it's time to deliver the unexpected. Yes, my friends, it's (drum roll, please) a weekend warrior recipe!

Randy's Bar Brawl Chili

Ingredients (for eight people, plus lots of leftovers):

A couple of packages of chili powder
Three pounds of burger meat
One pound of Italian sausage
Salt
Garlic
Two big-ass onions
Jalapeño peppers
Fifty-plus ounces of canned tomatoes (minced, if you can)
Beer
Thirty-plus ounces of kidney beans
Thirty-plus ounces of black beans
Ten-plus ounces of baked beans
Can o' corn
Half-empty Tupperware containers full of whatever

What you do:

1. Turn on sports radio and crack open a beer. Crumble one or two pounds of meat into a frying pan and cook over medium heat till somewhere between rare and medium rare. Dump fat into your empty beer can, put meat into a big pot. Cook the rest, repeating the whole process. With 95 percent of the fat drained off, but a

little left behind, brown diced onions, diced garlic, minced jalapeño peppers. Sprinkle some salt and the chili powder packets while browning. Yell at sports radio when a stupid caller comments on your team.

2. Remove sausage meat from its natural casing and crumble or dice. Brown as above.

3. Dump this mixture into the pot with the browned meat. At this point, your chili should look like Lambeau Field on a rainy day in early November, all brown and muddy!

4. Pour all of the canned tomatoes and corn into the pot, along with half a beer; a little more salt, too. Cheer sports radio host as he compliments your team.

5. Have one more chili packet and one more can of minced tomatoes at the ready so that you can season to taste. (Some garlic salt, Lee & Perrin's, Tabasco sauce, cumin, black pepper, Uncle Red's ashes, and/or crushed red pepper too.)

6. At this point, it's fun to check the fridge for leftovers. If it seems like it'd be decent—something like beef and Chinese vegetables, bacon bits, salsa, meatballs, the long-lost silicone implant of a Cowboys cheerleader, roasted peppers, whatever—throw it in there! Toast the update guy on the radio as he gives a clean bill of health to your quarterback for that day's game.

7. Heat under the pot should be less than medium but more than a simmer. Stir every ten minutes. After twenty minutes or so, you should be ready to chow down. Know, though, that the second tasting will be better than the first. Reheating brings out the juices. Or something culinary like that.

8. Don't forget to garnish with whatever you'd like (I dig cheese and Saltines). Also, drink that beer you toasted the update guy with. Everything tastes better after a beer.

Now, going out to watch a game is fine and good, but I truly believe that if you care about a sporting event, it's best viewed at home. I believe that like I believe that chili is healthy. With all my heart!

Chili on the couch is what Sundays are all about. Matty the dog thinks she just heard a duck . . .

Closing:
You're Never Too Old to
Count Three Mississippis

Let's say it's been fifteen years since you last played. Your arms have shriveled to string beans, your left knee is shot, your right eye wanders, and you couldn't hit Tony Siragusa's ass with a dart, let alone zing a football past a cornerback, if your life depended on it. Get down to the field anyway. You can still block somebody, can't you? You can still run a five-yard down and out? Count three Mississippis before rushing the passer? Draw up a play that actually works?

Well, then, quit making excuses!!!

Football is a physical game. I come home from those Saturday morning melees more sore than a port whore after the ship's come in. I mean it. The next morning, it's all I can do to roll out of bed, crawl across the floor to the rug, and then stretch enough so that I can trust my back in the shower. But my point—other than being able to rhyme "sore" and "whore"—is to describe the physical beauty of the game. And nothing embodies the speed and power of pigskin more than a man crawling to drain his bladder the morning after. Cook 'em, baby!

The hardest part is swallowing that pride; getting your overweight heinie up off of the couch that first morning; denying your inner couch potato and pulling on sweats and cleats in the middle of January (no air in the world smells better than winter air, my friend, so get out and breath it!); enduring the questioning look from your wife, kids, neighbor, boss, in-laws, and dog. They might think you're too old to play, but it just isn't true. Never forget that as of today you have 100 percent of your life left to live. Besides, the best guys I play with are the old-timers. They get more respect than anybody else. And if you're not old, well then, start playing now so that you can be one of those respectable elder statesmen once you are. Good habits are formed at a young age, but if that ship has sailed, fear not; old dogs can be taught new tricks!

That's all from this weekend warrior. I can only spend so much time with my hands on a keyboard and my ass in an office chair. I need to run a hook and ladder with my QB. I need to play a little man-to-man. I need to shoot the shit with the fellas. I need to feel sweat trickling down my back and the snow trying to force its way up. It's good for me. It's good for you. It's good for all of us. So, what're you waiting for? Isn't it time you got familiar with that most glorious of rhetorical questions: "One more trip up and back?" You bet your sweet safety blitz it is!

Bibliography

http://www.flagfootball.org/Flag%20Football%20Links.htm

http://www.footballresearch.com/

http://www.nfl.com/history

Juba, Kelvin. *Swimming for Fitness*. Guilford, Connecticut: The Lyons Press, 2002.

Kleiner, Susan M. and Greenwood-Robinson, Maggie. *High-Performance Nutrition*. New York: John Wiley & Sons, 1996.

Vickery, Donald M. and Fries, James F. *Take Care of Yourself*. Reading, Massachusetts: Addison-Wesley Publishing Company, Inc., 1992.